Critical Praise for
Do-It-Yourself Therapy

"This book has a voice that calls out to us from its pages, both encouraging and challenging us to hazard the biggest risk of all—that of changing ourselves."

> —Roslyn Duffy, counselor, teacher, and co-author of *Positive Discipline for Preschoolers* (Prima), *Positive Discipline: The First Three Years* (Prima), and *The Parent Report Card* (Parenting Press).

"Do-It-Yourself Therapy is lucid, practical, and engaging, and invites the reader to begin the journey towards positive personal growth and change. This book will also have immense value to therapists and other professionals interested in helping others achieve their goals."

> —Cheryl Erwin, MA, MFT, licensed marriage and family therapist, and co-author of four books in the *Positive Discipline* (Prima) parenting series.

"Insightful and to the point, this book will help you decide how to meet your personal challenges in a more healthy and helpful way."

> —Gary McKay, co-author of *How You Feel Is Up to You* (Impact)

"Does therapy have to be complicated? Does it have to be expensive? Can therapy be fun? No to the first two questions, and yes to the third with Do-It-Yourself Therapy. *You can even use this to start your own therapy group, and have even more fun while learning and growing."*

> —Jane Nelsen, Ed.D., co-author of the *Positive Discipline* (Prima) parenting series

Do-It-Yourself Therapy:

How To Think, Feel, and Act Like a New Person In Just 8 Weeks

By Lynn Lott,
Riki Intner,
and Barbara Mendenhall

CAREER
PRESS

Franklin Lakes, NJ

DO-IT-YOURSELF THERAPY
Cover design by Lu Rossman
Illustrations by Paula Gray
Printed in the U.S.A. by Book-mart Press

To order this title, please call toll-free 1-800-CAREER-1 (NJ and
Canada: 201-848-0310) to order using VISA or MasterCard, or for
further information on books from Career Press.

The Career Press, Inc., 3 Tice Road, PO Box 687, Franklin Lakes, NJ
07417

Library of Congress Cataloging-in-Publication Data

Lott, Lynn.
    Do it yourself therapy : how to think, feel, and act like a new
person in just 8 weeks / Lynn Lott, Riki Intner, and Barbara
Mendenhall.
        p.   cm.
    Includes index.
    ISBN 1-56414-409-7 (pbk.)
    1. Change (Psychology)   2. Attitude change.   I. Intner, Riki.
II. Mendenhall, Barbara.   III. Title.
BF637.C4L68   1999
158.1—dc21   99-25215
                                                                  CIP

Dedication

We dedicate this book to the many Adlerian/Dreikursian mentors who have introduced us to their creative applications of the principles of the Individual Psychology of Alfred Adler. We've lost track of the origin of so many of the ideas and tools that are now part of our daily practice, that it's sometimes impossible to give proper credit to everyone. If we forgot your name, it doesn't mean we forgot your contribution. We appreciate all of you.

Acknowledgements

More people contributed to the making of this book than we can possibly thank. We are grateful to all of you, and want to mention in particular...

Our many clients, family members, and friends for teaching us as much as you learned from using this material, for helping us develop and refine its use and presentation, and for allowing us to use your stories to help others by showing how you've grown and changed using these techniques.

Elisa Baker, for the thousand moments of simplicity and understanding your editing genius will afford the readers of the book.

Susan Madden for your help with theater metaphors.

Paula Gray for your inspirational ability to capture in a simple sketch the exact essence of what we want to illustrate. (She can be reached at jspirit@sonic.net if you wish to place an order.)

Sandee Gibson for your generosity and expertise in photography (sorry we missed the cover).

Adlerian authors who are helping parents throughout the world, including Don Dinkmeyer, Gary McKay, Michael Popkin, Linda Albert, Jane Nelsen, H. Steven Glenn, Roslyn Duffy, Cheryl Erwin, Frank Main, John Platt, Amy Lew, Betty Lou Bettner, and John Taylor.

Sheree Bykofsky for finding a home for this book.

Our husbands Hal Penny, John Amen, and Bob Intner, for more indulgence, support, and picking up of slack than we could have expected.

Ben Amen for the countless computer tricks you taught us making the writing process infinitely easier and your frantic mother considerably calmer.

Mim Pew, who never knew the monumental influence she would have when she gave us our first copy of *Children: The Challenge*.

Our children Corey and Casey Lott, Steven and David Penny, Jennifer, Samantha, David, and Sage Intner, and Jessica and Ben Amen for helping us "walk our talk," in order to teach others how to do the same.

And finally our editor, John J. O'Sullivan, for helping us create a much better book than what you started with.

Contents

Do-It-Yourself Therapy: Is It Possible?

There are two questions we are frequently asked. One is, "Can you really change your life in just eight weeks?" And the second is, "If it only takes eight weeks to change your life, why are we in therapy with you for months or years?" Both are excellent questions! We thought of the time each of us had started something new and realized how quickly our lives began to change once we reached a turning point. For everyone, there are turning points. These turning points are moments when you become a *new* person engaged in growth. Reading *Do-It-Yourself Therapy* can be a turning point for you. Your life can change, whether you work your way through every chapter and activity, or pick and choose the ones that appeal to you.

We have found that changes are short-lived if you don't incorporate them into your life. Our book can be transforming if you are willing to devote time to its activities on a regular basis. We know that somewhere in the eight weeks you will find yourself thinking, feeling, and acting differently—We trust that you will find the path that will lead to lifelong change.

Barbara first started attending a Family Education Center drop-in parent support group in 1984. It only took one visit to realize that she could make changes—she felt an immediate sense of hope. At first, she modified her relationship with her child. Later, she recognized the ripple effect on her relationships with other people, including her husband, her business associates, and her friends. She stopped mentally assigning everyone she knew to one of two categories: Those who had something to teach her and those who didn't interest her. When she began to look for the unique value and strengths in everyone, she felt more optimistic, joyful, and connected. Barbara attended the parenting program regularly, enrolled in the two-year-long parent educator training program, worked as a parent educator, and eventually became executive director of the organization.

For Riki, buying her first computer was a major turning point in her life. She found out she could learn skills that she had thought impossible. Before the computer, Riki stopped herself if she thought an activity would be too difficult and overwhelming. After the computer she realized that she could take tasks on step-by-step, and work at a level that was comfortable for her. She discovered that she doesn't have to know more than three programs to enjoy using her computer. To her amazement, Riki found out that using the computer could be fun. When her daughter moved to Paris, they kept in touch with each other via e-mail. Maybe you'll approach *Do-It-Yourself Therapy* like Riki, by not becoming an expert, but by picking and choosing what works to make your life easier and more fun.

Lynn recently started attending her daughter's Wednesday night yoga class, which has become a major turning point for her. The very first class changed Lynn's life—she realized she had muscles that hadn't been used since she was eight! Because quality of life is extremely important to Lynn, she committed to do what she could, knowing that small steps were better than no steps at all. At first, all she did was attend class once a week. Now she has purchased some yoga tapes and has begun practicing at home between classes. She knows that even if it takes her several years to increase the level of her practice, she feels stronger, has less aches and pains, and is more aware of her body. Then there's the added pleasure of enjoying time with her daughter.

You may choose to use our material the same way that Lynn approached yoga—beginning with awareness of the changes you want to make, then taking one small step after another, continuing to practice as the new approach becomes an expanding part of your life. Personal growth is exciting work and an important investment in yourself. How long it takes and how hard you work is an individual matter. We trust that this book will lead to lifelong change.

Be Your Own Therapist

C an all problems be resolved by self-therapy in eight weeks? Wouldn't someone who has been diagnosed with a personality disorder or another psychiatric condition need some serious professional help, in addition to working through self-discovery? And if it only takes eight weeks to really change your life, why do people stay in therapy for weeks, months, or even years? All of these are excellent questions.

In *Do-It-Yourself Therapy,* we help you help yourself by offering information, effective tools, skills, and encouragement that you can use to find solutions to real-life problems. Our emphasis is twofold: do it yourself, because with help and guidance you *can* do it yourself, and change yourself, because the only person you can change is you.

Growing and changing with the help of a caring guide is therapeutic. You can be your own guide and enrich your life by using this book instead of going to a therapist. Or, if you are seeing a therapist, our book can enhance your work together. For those of you who participate in self-help groups, use our book as a manual along with your group work. If you are a therapist, you'll find considerable material in this book to use with your clients.

As you read through the book, you'll notice that our focus is different from many current self-help models. We do not look for causes or for blame. Instead of looking at problems as someone else's fault or as something physiologically wrong with you, we'll show you how problems are primarily about relationships, including the most important relationship you have—the one with yourself.

You may feel relieved to see a different way to understand behavior. Others may find our approach overly simplistic. Don't let that stop you. We suggest that you suspend judgement as you read. Instead of looking at the material as positive or negative, right or wrong, good or bad, treat it as interesting information that can help you move forward in your life.

Ours is an eight-week, step-by-step approach that is both user-friendly and easy to understand. You can start at the beginning or simply open to a topic of your choice. You don't have to read the sections in order, but do read **all** the sections. Each one has different, important information that will increase your self-awareness, help you replace self-defeating patterns, and transform your relationships.

Use our eight-week plan to get to the root of your problems and make changes that will bring happiness and satisfaction to your life. Because there are so many choices and so much helpful information presented each week, we suggest recycling through the eight weeks often. Each time you do, you'll see more new possibilities to strengthen yourself.

Each week, you'll be introduced to information and stories about real people. Each will expand your awareness and solve the mystery of why you and others behave the way you do. You'll find ideas that provide you with one "ah ha" experience after another. You may hear yourself saying, "I never thought of that before."

People do three things: They think, they feel, and they do. People also make changes in the same three ways. Some do it by shifting their thinking, or by adjusting their attitude. Others need an action plan to do things differently. Then there are those who don't make any changes until they deal with their feelings. *Do-It-Yourself Therapy* offers a holistic approach to better relationships by considering all of you. Whether you think it, feel it, or do it, each small step you take will help you feel better and do better.

How did I become who I am?

Your authors are students of the psychology of Alfred Adler and Rudolf Dreikurs. Alfred Adler and Rudolf Dreikurs were the fathers of modern psychology. Adler (1870–1937) had radically different thinking about human nature and motivation than his contemporaries. He and his student, Rudolf Dreikurs embraced concepts of social equality, mutual respect, encouragement, holism, and human potential. They engineered ideas and techniques that are now familiar to practitioners everywhere, though they are rarely credited. (The three of us have studied, practiced, and lived their philosophy since the late 60s and are indebted to the many Adlerians who have shared their ideas and interpretations with us over the years.)

Our core belief rests upon personal decisions. It's not what happened in your life that shaped your personality but what you consciously and unconsciously decided about those events and/or circumstances. Many of these decisions were made in your childhood (before you were 5 years old). Picture going for a ride in a car with a 5-year-old behind the wheel. Most of us are living our adult lives in this way. You may be surprised to find out just how much influence that child inside of you has.

This book will help you get out of this "emotional kindergarten" once and for all. As you read the following stories, notice how the underlying unconscious decisions made in childhood are running these people's lives today. Then, think about how you are still operating like a little kid.

Jimmy's story

Jimmy was very upset with his boss, who didn't seem to appreciate his work or effort. Jimmy worked very hard, and when his boss didn't say anything about his work, he worked harder and longer hours. The boss didn't seem to notice, so Jimmy complained to his friends after work and added more hours to his day. Naturally, this didn't solve his problem.

As a child, when Jimmy didn't understand something in school and wanted the teacher to help him out, he did almost the same thing, with the same result. Clearly, Jimmy hadn't updated the coping methods he used in elementary school, even though he was now in his forties.

Nikki's story

Nikki wanted to be picked to be the Easter bunny at the school's Easter party. She thought it would be fun to wear the costume with the cute ears and fluffy tail and to give out candies to everyone from the brightly colored Easter basket. The day the children got to volunteer for jobs for the party, Nikki was home, sick with the flu. When she returned to school and saw the list of children chosen for the party, she cried, as someone else was signed up to be the Easter bunny. She sat in her chair and cried so hard that the teacher sent her to the nurse's office. Feeling embarrassed and hurt, Nikki told the nurse she wasn't feeling well and wanted to go home. Her parents picked her up and took home. She stayed home for several days feigning illness. Finally, her parents sent her back to school, never knowing what was really upsetting their daughter. Nikki held on to her resentment and refused to have any fun at the Easter party.

As an adult, when things get hard for Nikki, she stays away from work, classes, or friends because she is "sick." Then, she waits for someone to fix things and make her feel better, even though no one knows what is going on. Nikki thinks everyone should know why she is really upset and do something about it.

Like Jimmy or Nikki, if life doesn't match your expectations, you experience stress. The greater the gap between your "shoulds" and how life really is, the greater the stress. The more stressed you are, the more likely you are to rely on your inner child's decisions.

Peeling off labels

Another way to find out what you learned in "emotional kindergarten" is to think about the labels you got when you were younger. Were you the "difficult child," the "smart one," the "athlete," or the "family clown?" Are you still acting out those childhood labels as an adult?

()Hint Try this

Here's a little test to show you how easy it is to use outdated relationship skills:

Think about a recent situation when you were feeling unloved or dissatisfied. Any situation will work to help you learn how you go about trying to solve problems and get your way as an adult. What was happening in that recent situation?

What were other people doing? What were you doing? Was that helping to solve the problem? Now think about how you went about getting your way as a child.

Did you pout, whine, demand, sulk, have temper tantrums, argue, yell, name call, or attack? Did you try to do exactly what was expected of you and strive to please others in order to "earn" what it was you wanted? Do you notice any similarities between what you were doing in the recent situation and the behavior you used as a child? Were you using any of those methods you honed before you were five to try to get your way recently as an adult? How well were they working and how did you feel about yourself?

As a child, you compared yourself to others constantly. If you decided you didn't measure up, you may have given up an important part of yourself. Maybe you tried to overcompensate to be "good enough." Do you always have to be a *certain* way—be it difficult, smart, funny, or the opposite of others—to be "good" enough? Or do you think that because you aren't a certain way that you aren't good enough? If you do, it's that little kid in you who tells you life is this black and white. Reading this book will help you break through your stereotypes and prejudices about yourself so you can gain a different perspective and be your own best catalyst for change.

How to use this book

As you read each chapter, think about specific relationships you want to change. Then, use the section at the end of each chapter called **Creating Changes in Your World** to develop a plan you can use to help improve that relationship. Start by looking through the **Obstacles to Growth and Change** to see how you might trip yourself up during the week. You can avoid many of these pitfalls simply by becoming aware of them.

Next, pick out one or two suggestions from **Easy Steps for Change** and write them down. You may find that keeping records in a journal works well for you. Or you might prefer to use post-it notes and stick them on a bathroom mirror or the refrigerator to help you stay focused during the week.

Finally, take the time to do the **Activities**. These will help you translate this information into actions that work. If you use a journal to record your answers, you can refer back to the information from time to time to jog your memory or see how much you've changed. As you take one small step and work one small thing about yourself at a time, you may be surprised to find yourself changing dramatically in other ways as well!

If I had only known this...

You can't change without a picture and you can't do what you don't know how to do. *Do-It-Yourself Therapy* gives you information to help you improve your life dramatically. We offer suggestions for your relationship with yourself and your intimate others, as well as for parenting, work life, extended family, and friendships.

In Week 1, you'll learn about the process of change so you can have a realistic view of how change really happens. Change starts with desire, which you already have—you're reading this book. Lasting change requires self-acceptance, as well as a picture of how you want to be. We'll show you step-by-step how to get there.

In Week 2 you'll discover how you stop yourself from making positive change by being protective when you feel stressed and fearful. We call these four protective styles "top cards." You'll learn how to identify your top card, find out how you learned to play it, what happens when you do it, and what you can do instead in order to break down your resistance to change by facing your fears.

In Week 3, we'll show you how playing your top card affects your primary relationships, what some typical top card relationship combinations are, and ways to make changes on a daily basis that invite more cooperative and less combative relationships.

During Week 4, you'll look at how you got to be the person you are today and how to accept yourself for who you are. Your childhood relationships and experiences, and the decisions and conclusions you made about them, helped you shape your personality. By increasing your awareness of those childhood decisions about self, others and life, you'll have a chance to discard or change those decisions which may be creating problems for you and replace them with decisions that will help you live life more fully.

In Week 5, by showing you more about how your past impacts your present relationships, we continue taking you backwards...so you can move forward. You'll learn how to use early childhood memories to identify and work with the decisions you made as a child (called your private logic), see how those decisions may be keeping you stuck, and become aware of new ways to operate today. Early memory work gives you keys that help you unlock the door to your past so you can access the wealth of information inside you and use the information constructively.

Then in Week 6, you'll learn a new way of thinking about behavior. Instead of looking for its causes, you'll see how to identify the purpose of behavior, to understand how discouragement creates mischief, and how to move toward attitudes and actions that are more encouraging to yourself and others. Using proactive, healthy ways of meeting four basic needs, you can move from the normal reactive responses, that keep you stuck and give you problems, to constructive actions that help you and others accomplish recognition, power, justice, and skills. The activities this week will help you use your feelings to identify other people's discouragement as well as your own, and decide how to encourage yourself and others.

Week 7 is all about discovering the connection and differences between what you think, what you feel, and what you do. You'll be amazed at how easy it is to change yourself and reverse the problems of relationships once you understand how you create the patterns that sometimes keep you stuck. You'll learn how to feel your feelings instead of think your feelings, how the mind and body connect, how your thoughts can create disease, and how to create action plans that help you make changes now.

In Week 8 you'll learn how to maintain healthier relationships. After learning what a relationship is and what constitutes "healthy," you'll have an opportunity to assess your own relationships and discover techniques for increasing "social interest" in your life. By learning the difference between horizontal, cooperative, and mutually respectful relationships, versus vertical, discouraging, and competitive relationships, you'll be able to identify what's lacking in your important relationships and how you can improve them.

There is no quick fix!

There are many books in print today with titles like *Computers for Dummies, Spanish for Morons,* and even *Car Mechanics for Dunces.* They are popular because they make complex subjects simple and offer steps that are easy to follow. That's what the three of us do with our clients. It's what this book *Do-It-Yourself Therapy* is all about. Whether you're feeling stuck, depressed, or would like someone to fix your husband, wife, children, in-laws, or (you fill in the blank) and send them back when they're "done," this book can give you the kind of help we provide our clients in individual therapy.

You probably didn't learn the information in our book at home or at school, and many times, you aren't exposed to this information as an adult. People in our society are often looking for the quick fix, the one thing that will change everything instantly, instead of using therapy to gain a more in-depth understanding of how their quality of life depends upon the health and satisfaction in all their relationships, especially the relationship with themselves. You are a complex person and it took many years to form your personality.

Change is a process. Our eight-week plan helps you begin a pattern of self-empowerment that will lead you to healthier relationships and change your life. You need only trust the process and move forward one step at a time, at your own pace. By the time you finish *Do-It-Yourself Therapy,* you'll be in the driver's seat of your own life.

 **Week 1**

Discover How Change Happens

C ontrary to what you believe, only you have the power to change your life. In order to accomplish this, you must be willing to do the work to change yourself. Only then can you make permanent transformations in your life and your relationships. Depression, pain, anxiety, sadness, suicidal feelings, chemical dependency, and other difficulties do not have to be permanent conditions. You do not have to spend the rest of your life feeling miserable or sorry for yourself.

In this first week of work, you will learn to believe in yourself. You will be able to create experiences of self-discovery and self-acceptance. You'll get a jump-start to approaching your life with courage, confidence, and optimism. You will create action plans for your future success. It's important here not to slow your progress by trying to fix someone else, by waiting for others to change, or by looking to place blame. Unless you adjust your thoughts, your feelings, or your actions, you'll continue to end up in the same situations you wish to avoid.

It doesn't matter where you start

If you are the kind of person who likes to understand the reason for everything and uses logic to solve problems, the vignettes and information in this book will help you readjust your thoughts. As you grasp how and why relationships work and gain insights into your unconscious beliefs, change will be possible.

Maybe you're the type of person who changes by experiencing, accepting, or expressing your feelings. Think of all the times others have tried to help you fix your circumstances, or have reasoned with you endlessly to get you to be different. However, nothing changed until it felt safe for you to have your feelings. This book contains stories and activities that will help you make changes by dealing with your feelings.

If you change by taking action and just want to know what to do, the **Creating Changes in Your World** section of each chapter will give you many action suggestions in addition to the other "to-do" ideas sprinkled throughout the chapters. Thoughts, feelings, and actions are interconnected. Therapy happens when you make changes in one of these areas, which will change the others as well. When you change your actions, your thoughts about yourself change. When you feel better, you will do better.

No matter what your style of change, at some point, you need to try things out in the real world to practice your new skills. This is a big part of *Do-It-Yourself Therapy*, so be sure to work carefully through the **Creating Changes in Your World** section at the end of each chapter. Take the time to use the suggestions for planning to improve a specific relationship.

Robert's story

Robert's story is an example of one person who began making changes at his own pace. Robert felt awkward and was quiet in social gatherings.

Hint   Let yourself be a learner

Can you remember when you were in kindergarten? You were just beginning, and there were no expectations. We'd like you to adopt the same attitude about changing yourself now. You're exactly where you should be: at the beginning.

Let yourself be a beginner and a learner, expanding your growth step by step. Remind yourself that you are just fine the way you are and that your self-worth isn't conditional on whether you make changes perfectly or quickly. Take the pressure off. Honor your pace and style for making changes in your life.

The more anxious he felt, the quieter he got. When he finally spoke, he stuttered and groped for the right word, until everyone seemed to lose interest in the conversation. He was certain that when people interrupted him, changed the subject, or walked off to get an hors d'oeuvre, it was because they were bored with him. Robert wanted to feel relaxed and included in social situations. After all, he was expected to attend the frequent employee gatherings.

As Robert began identifying his inner thoughts, he discovered that when he thought he was socially inadequate, he felt anxious. He could see that he was comparing himself to others and that he was ruining his own fun because he wasn't measuring up. His belief was that everyone else was confident and only he was nervous. It never occurred to him that others might also be as uncomfortable as he was, but that they handled their discomfort differently. Since he never checked out his perceptions, the only advice and counsel he got was from himself. This self-deception kept him stuck in his mistaken thought patterns.

Robert decided to take action and check out his beliefs, instead of mulling them over again in his head. One day he asked his handball partner Ted, a colleague whom he saw chatting up a storm at company functions, how he always managed to be so at ease. Ted laughed. He said that he and his wife had just been talking about that very topic. His wife had observed that when he's nervous and self-conscious at parties, Ted jabbers and monopolizes conversations. But Ted told Robert he notices that when his wife is anxious, she stays near the buffet table and nibbles all evening, something she never does at home.

Once he was aware that not everything others did at a party was a response to him, Robert felt calm. Robert was astonished to learn that some of the least anxious-looking people were as ill at ease as he was. He saw that he was mistaken in thinking their actions were caused by what he said or did, and that instead, they were probably acting out of their own discomfort.

Ted helped Robert further by telling him some of the tricks he'd learned over the years to better cope in social gatherings. For instance, if he caught himself before he started to blather, he explained, he could remind himself to focus on and be interested in what others had to say. Then, he could be curious and ask questions. Ted explained that most people really enjoy talking about themselves. When he could remember to give them a chance to express themselves, he usually felt more relaxed. Conversations flowed more naturally, and he was genuinely interested in what others were thinking and feeling, instead of worrying about how he was coming across.

Robert took to heart the "secrets" Ted had shared, and he worked on making his own changes, and he felt more encouraged, he wasn't able to change his social life overnight. That's not how change happens for Robert or anyone else, as change is a continuous process.

The 4 steps of the change process

There are four steps involved in making changes. These are: desire, awareness, acceptance, and options. If you read a book, take a class, join a group, look up the number for a 12-step program, call a therapist, or simply tell another person you want to make some changes, you have begun. Even though someone might tell you that you need help or that you need to change, change doesn't really start until you have the **desire** to make your life better. By reading this book, you have begun the change process. You are at step one: desire.

We often talk with our clients about the second step, **awareness**, in terms of "A.C." and "B.C.," or after consciousness and before consciousness. Moving from B.C. to A.C. is like being in a dark room and then having someone turn on the light. Until you're conscious and aware of your patterns of thinking, feeling, and behaving, you cannot begin to change them. When you work with a therapist, someone other than you is able to help you see things that are often difficult to see for yourself. *Do-It-Yourself Therapy* will help you become more self-aware.

People seem to find **acceptance**, the third step the most difficult to accomplish. Acceptance is the ability to separate your thoughts, feelings, and actions from your self-worth. You are able to say, "This is how (it, he, she, I, life) is; it's a fact, not a judgment, it's simply information." Acceptance means focusing on reality (what is) instead of the past (what was)

(!) Hint   Change is a process, not a destination

If you find yourself feeling discouraged that change isn't happening fast enough, remind yourself that in therapy, change is a process, not a destination.

There is no finish line, so your choice is how you take the journey.

Take small steps, encourage yourself, and pat yourself on the back for your efforts; it may seem painfully slow, but it beats waiting for the world to change around you.

or the future (what might be). You can stop comparing, criticizing, and judging yourself, or thinking you are worthless.

Without acceptance, change can only be temporary. Sometimes it helps to pretend there is an encouraging voice whispering in your ear that you are good enough just the way you are. If you hear yourself responding to that voice with "yes, buts" and "if onlys," you're not there yet. When you accept yourself as you are, you begin "catching yourself," instead of beating up on yourself. You will notice one of your ineffective behaviors after you've done it, as you're doing it, or on occasion, before you're about to begin.

From here, the last step in the change process follows quite naturally. Once you become more accepting of yourself, you'll begin discovering that the world is full of **options**. As you focus less on your mistakes or on impressing others, you'll be more open to trying new thoughts and behaviors.

Marcus' story

After many unhappy years, Marcus' father eventually took his own life. Drugs, shock treatments, inpatient help, or any of his family's efforts did nothing to lighten his depression. Marcus wondered if this meant he might end up doing the same thing his father had. He also feared for his teenage son—was there a genetic fault in his family? For Marcus the first step, **desire**, came when he decided to get some help, to deal with his guilt and pain about the loss of his father, as well as keeping him from getting his father's "illness."

Marcus thought it was his fault that his father had died. He thought if he had been a better son, that this wouldn't have happened. He took the step to **awareness** with help from do-it-yourself therapy. He realized what he really feared was loss of control. He couldn't stop his father from killing himself, and he feared that it might happen again with one of his own children. In this fear, he was trying to control his son's life and make sure nothing "bad" happened. He knew this was ridiculous, but he still believed that he was responsible for everyone's actions.

The third step, **acceptance**, was very difficult for Marcus. He thought that accepting the situation meant he was accepting his father's suicide. When Marcus began to see that acceptance simply meant recognizing his own self-accusation as well as acknowledging the fact that he couldn't have stopped the suicide, he began to change. No amount of "if onlys" changed anything. Once Marcus accepted this, he was able to move on.

Marcus had a friend who was a handwriting analyst. When his friend saw how upset Marcus was, he offered to interpret his father's suicide note. Marcus gained a better understanding of what his father was feeling at the time of his suicide. On examination, the handwriting showed that his father was a very proud man, a man who kept his feelings to himself, and didn't want to be a burden to others—especially his children. He was an independent person whose suicide was his means of choosing his own exit. This analysis helped free Marcus, allowing him to work toward acceptance. He understood, with his friend's help, that his father didn't want to change, and Marcus could have done nothing to stop him.

Once Marcus stopped blaming himself, he was able to grieve the loss of his father and begin to see **options**. He stopped trying to "rescue" his son. Instead of worrying that he carried and passed down a genetic predisposition for suicide, Marcus realized a more productive option would be to let his son handle his own life's difficulties. With respect to himself, Marcus learned he was a very different person than his father, and he would approach the challenges of his life and death in his own way.

Change can be difficult

We realize change is difficult. Change often involves taking two steps forward and one step back. Think of change in terms of learning a new language, sport, or musical instrument. At first you feel awkward and uncomfortable and it's hard to see any progress. Later, you may see the progress you have made, but you still have to concentrate on every move you make. It's only after a lot of practice that the new skill becomes natural.

If you're like most people, you may think it's not fair that you have to work so hard at making changes. It's only human nature to want others to change first. We all drag our feet about actually doing something constructive to make our life work better. Some people call not wanting to change "resistance," but we prefer to call it "human nature." Old habits and thought patterns are hard to break.

One difference between an adult and a child is that a child is scientific. He or she tries something out. If it doesn't work, the child tries something else. An adult, on the other hand, will try something out. If it doesn't work, he or she will do the same thing over and over, hoping to get a different result. If an adult is attempting to change someone else, he or she may even give a little history lesson, saying, "If I've told you once, I've told you a thousand times," or, "How many times do I have to show you how to...." In addition to years of practice at repeating patterns that don't work, you may also have a lot at stake in staying the way you are.

Don's story

Don was the kid in his family who everyone said never ate vegetables or fruit. He got a lot of attention for refusing to eat certain things and soon his list of forbidden foods got bigger and bigger. Eventually, his family referred to him as the "Pickiest Eater in the World." Don was not about to give up that title easily—for whatever reason, it made him feel special and important. Don reported that when he went away to college and no one cared whether he ate or not, it became easier for him to try new foods. However, breaking the habit on the home front was too hard.

Your changes impact everyone

Just because you decide you want to change does not mean the people around you will feel comfortable when you act differently. They may try to get you to go back to your old behaviors out of their fear. They may even make it very hard for you to be different by criticizing you, building alliances behind your back, or by using emotional blackmail, emotional abuse, or threats. Sometimes you might think it would be easier to go back to your old habits because others are not pleased or are not making their own changes fast enough. When the people around

(!) Hint   A desire to change...or a desire *not* to change?

Try this easy experiment to see for yourself what we mean. Clasp your hands, interlacing your fingers, and look at which of your thumbs is on top. Now separate your hands and put them back together with the opposite thumb on top. Hold this position for a minute and notice what is happening in your body.

Are you uncomfortable? Do you want to return to the first, familiar position? This same discomfort and tendency to go back to the familiar will probably happen when you try out the suggestions in this book. Don't worry. It's just your brain impulses and ingrained patterns trying to catch up with your new desire.

You will get better at whatever you practice. Remind yourself that this won't always feel uncomfortable. Give yourself permission to continue moving forward. Congratulate yourself on practicing your new thoughts, feelings, and actions.

you get uncomfortable right along with you, hold firm in spite of their discomfort. Just because you are changing doesn't mean everyone else will be happy about it or be willing to change. The only person you can change is yourself. The more you improve your skills and attitudes, the more you invite cooperation from others.

Margaret's story

Margaret struggled with her sexuality for many years, and after much soul searching, therapy, and experimentation, realized she was a lesbian. For her, it was both a relief and an obstacle. She began dating women and felt better about herself than she had in years. At the same time, she worried more and more about what to tell her parents, who she believed would never tolerate her preference because of their religious beliefs. While her father was alive, Margaret could not bring herself to tell him the truth. A year after her father died, she decided it was time to be honest with her mother. Margaret hated the deception, was feeling alienated from her family, and wanted to introduce her mom to Alicia, her partner of almost a year. She was used to protecting her mother from the truth or pretending to do what her parents wanted in order to keep the peace. After working hard to be open and honest about her sexuality, she no longer had patience for falsehood and lies.

In a gut-wrenching conversation, Margaret "came out" to her mother and told her about her partner. Although Margaret knew it would be difficult, she had not prepared herself for the response she got. Though she believed her mother would not cut her off or condemn her to hell, she had thought they would be able to have a conversation. Instead, her mother quoted the Bible about the evils of homosexuality and insisted that Margaret would grow out of this.

Instead of trying to convince her mother to change her mind or retreating into her old ways of compliance or sneakiness, Margaret said, "Mom, I love you and I know this is very shocking information. I don't expect you to understand or embrace what I'm doing, especially with so little time to process it, but I want you to know that I won't be changing my decision about my sexuality, the door is always open for you and I to talk about this and your feelings about it. I hope we will be able to stay friends and spend time together."

Her mother thought for a moment and said, "I really need some time. Don't bring your friend to my birthday party next week. It's too soon for me. I love you and I want to stay close to you, but I am just not sure what I can do. Just let me see."

Learn to take small steps

Margaret understood that just because she had changed, did not mean everyone around her would change as well. She resisted thinking too far into the future, having unrealistic goals, or attaching too much energy to the end result. She knew these were good ways to get stuck and make change difficult. Yet, she knew she had to take some step if she wanted to have a relationship with her mother. If you are not getting started because your goals seem like impossible dreams, zero in on a reasonable first step, like the small step Doug and Danielle discovered.

Doug and Danielle's story

Doug and Danielle started using the ideas in *Do-It-Yourself Therapy* after doing some goal-setting with an expensive consultant to help them figure out how they could spend more time traveling, which they both enjoyed. After all the time and money they spent, they were still disappointed because nothing had changed, even though they now had a long list of options. Doug was frustrated because he believed that the things on their list were too expensive. When Doug said they couldn't afford to do the things on their list, Danielle was angry because after all they had done, nothing had changed.

Arguing over travel was taking a serious toll on their relationship. They questioned whether they could meet their individual needs, and still be together. After working with the ideas in this book, Doug and Danielle realized they were asking the wrong question—the problem wasn't whether to stay together or leave, but how to limit their choices.

In the past they got stuck when Danielle suggested they take more vacations and worry about the money later. Doug refused to travel until they had the money saved. What they finally came up with was so simple that they both laughed. First they agreed on the country they would both like to travel to and then they looked at a map of that country. They called a travel agent and asked for information on places of interest, tours and airfares. They both were excited about this step. The idea of limiting their effort had never occurred to either of them before, and without a new picture, it was impossible to make a change. Sometimes a thoroughly accomplished single small step allows everything else to fall into place. The road to change is paved with small steps.

We find that people have unrealistic expectations about how change happens. They give up because they think it's taking too long or it's too much work. They don't know that things often get worse before they get better and that stopping at the hard part is the wrong place to quit.

Looking for the quick fix

Another way to make change difficult is to look for a quick fix—one that will change everything. In therapy, some of the more popular quick fixes these days are pharmacological: antidepressants, pain killers, tranquilizers, sleeping pills, among others. This kind of short-term fix will not only leave you with your original symptoms, but it may also mask your real problems and create damaging side effects. It's often a matter of time before you feel worse than when you started. Be suspicious of methods that promise miracle cures. A shocking number of health care providers now pull out their prescription pads without much conversation, as soon as they hear a patient say, "I'm depressed."

Depression is not a disease. Depression can be either one of the many feelings humans experience-or it can also be a constellation of thoughts, feelings, and behaviors, which turn into a paralyzing discouragement. You are not diseased, and you can change using the methods outlined in our book.

Some of you may be thinking "Is this medically accurate? My doctor told me that this is 'clinical' depression. One day it just came out of nowhere and *BAM*, one morning I couldn't get out of bed. I eventually discovered much of it had to do with problems in my developing years but without medicine, I don't see how could have started getting better." It may seem to you that you were hit with a disease. However, if you had gotten help sooner exploring your underlying issues, you may have never experienced that sudden attack. If you stop thinking of your problems as diseases and keep reading, you will discover a model to help you get to the root of your problems...without destructive chemical solutions.

In *The California Therapist*, July/August 1995, Ilana Singer, M.S., reports on an interview with Peter Breggin, M.D., a Harvard-trained psychiatrist, former consultant to National Institute of Mental Health (N.I.M.H.), and George Mason University professor. She writes, "...often without questioning whether the benefits outweigh the risks, millions of Americans take psychoactive drugs prescribed by their primary care physician or psychiatrist." Dr. Breggin argues that the brain-damaging effects of these chemical treatments are being ignored and are far more dangerous than people realize. Critical of "quick-fix" biopsychiatrists who call psychosocial and community treatment approaches "old-fashioned," Breggin documents the hazards of what he calls the "New Psychiatry," and asserts that "mental illness" is not biological or genetic in origin. We couldn't agree more, and suggest that you read his books for an in-depth look at the effects of biopsychiatric intrusions.

Maybe you're already taking Zoloft, Prozac, or Xanax, and are afraid to stop. After all, your doctor prescribed them. If you are using antidepressants, we encourage you to work on the deeper issues that brought you to this point, and wean yourself from the drugs as you strengthen your relationship skills. There are many physicians who will support you in this choice. In his interview with Ilana Singer, Dr. Breggin says, "Psychiatric drugs, if they're not doing brain damage, are at least causing brain dysfunction which is not the side effect, it's the primary effect." (page 54 of *The California Therapist*, July/August, 1995).

We have clients who believe that using medication along with therapy is the course that is best for them. Using drug-free methods, we have been able to help many clients who have been previously diagnosed with conditions for which medication is traditionally prescribed. Yet we know that some of you reading this book will be resistant to changing your thinking about the need for medication. Our job is to provide you with choices and help you see other routes to change so you can help yourself. But, we believe that ultimately *you* are the person who knows you best. If using drugs is your choice, we hope you will look for suggestions in our book that will augment your current therapy and make your life work better. We hope that drugs can be a transitional step and not a lifetime habit.

Have the courage to fail...and try again

If you have given up on yourself and believe that you can't change, you have lost your courage. Courage is the knowledge that you can make a mistake, and it won't be the end of the world. You can deal with what comes your way and you can try again. If you can't make it different on the 100th try, you might need to experiment one more time—the 101st time could be the charm. It takes a tremendous amount of courage and a sense of humor to tackle changing your lifelong patterns and attitudes. When you do make a mistake (and *you will* if you're human), what matters is what you learn from it, and what you do about it then.

Courage is something you can build in small steps by following the suggestions in this book, and that's how you can get yourself moving forward again and believing in yourself. At some point, all of us need courage to face the biggest change of all: We all have to grow up. Perhaps you think that as you grow older everything will fall into place automatically. But growing older isn't the same as growing up. You need to actively participate in making your life happier and healthier. It is **never** too late to start changing and growing up, but it is much harder to do so without a blueprint.

Healthy change is about growing up

When people come to us for therapy, part of our job is to help them grow up, as every problem involves a snag in the growth process. During growth, most people missed out on attaining independence. Without independence, they cannot become interdependent. Interdependence is an essential step towards becoming a whole person with healthy, relationships. We help our clients "grow up" by keeping them on the path of change.

Our map depicts a path from the total **dependence** on others you have at birth, to **independence**, where you are capable of meeting your own emotional and physical needs and are aware of who you are. From independence you can move to **interdependence**, where you cooperate with others, sharing tasks and supporting each other. When you follow our map, you will stop letting other people run your life. You can learn to decide for yourself what you think, feel, and will do. You *can* make your life work.

Shelly's story

Very few people were raised according to our map. Shelly's experience might help you see more clearly how childhood training can influence current problems.

When Shelly was a young child, every time she made a move to think for herself—from deciding what to wear when she got up in the morning to how she spent her birthday money—she was criticized, corrected, and instructed to do things the "right way." The "right way," according to her parents, was their way. Her parents didn't know how to encourage her independence, nor did they want to. They may have been simply practicing the parenting style of their day. Perhaps they were afraid of encouraging her independence because they thought it might mean they were neglecting Shelly, not showing love if they didn't oversee all aspects of her life.

An adolescent's age-appropriate task is to "individuate"; to figure out how he or she thinks and feels. When Shelly started this process, her parents panicked, and pulled their reins tighter, keeping her dependent on them. They were afraid she would do something stupid or dangerous. They convinced her that they knew what was best for her.

Some children become rebellious when this happens. Others, like Shelly, become submissive. She gave in to her parents and ignored any thoughts and feelings that disagreed with theirs. She lost confidence in her decisions. She believed that someone else always knew better.

As an adult, she continued this pattern of dependence, choosing relationships with people who would tell her what to do and how to think. She was afraid to trust her own thoughts and feelings, as she believed she was being selfish or hurtful, especially if others disagreed. She also didn't realize that her parents and partners had their own fears and insecurities. They feared that if Shelly became more independent, she wouldn't need them. She might leave and never come back.

With so much of her energy expended to keep others happy, Shelly could not grow up and achieve independence. As time went on, she remained a child in an adult's body, struggling to deal with the problems in the adult world. She didn't have the self-confidence or skills needed to cope. She felt scared, angry, and depressed, but she held it all inside and began experiencing panic attacks. To win back her own life, Shelly

---

(!) Hint   How to have a really bad day

Faulty thinking isn't limited to believing mistakes are disasters. We often tease our clients by saying, "If you want to have a really bad day, try one of these exercises in futility. We promise they'll sap your courage and demolish your self-esteem."

POST THIS
HOW TO HAVE A REALLY BAD DAY!

- ☑ Compare yourself to others.
- ☑ Judge yourself.
- ☑ Think in concrete absolutes (either/or, black or white).
- ☑ Make every catastrophy bigger and worse than it is.
- ☑ Worry about problems you don't have yet.
- ☑ Refuse to face reality; live in fantasy.
- ☑ Practice negative self-talk.
- ☑ Think that it's a crime to make a mistake.
- ☑ Believe that you're nobody...unless you're perfect.

needed to find a way to become more independent, as well as to learn to become interdependent.

Is it time for you to wean yourself from dependency and begin changing by becoming more independent? See how Shelly did it by using our map.

Shelly learns to follow our map

Shelly attended a workshop where she could practice changing her behavior in a safe setting. She invited her boyfriend Alex to join her. In this workshop, the participants were asked to try out some activities that simulate different types of relationships.

We were first introduced to these activities at a workshop put on by John Taylor, an Adlerian therapist from Salem, Oregon. In this workshop, he showed us how to help people learn "experientially." His exercises show that when people learn from their hearts, instead of their heads, they learn faster and retain information longer. (You can obtain many experiential activities in the training manuals written by Lynn Lott and Jane Nelsen. Call [800]456-7770 for a catalog.)

The first activity demonstrated how dependent adults relate to each other. Following the moderator's directions, Alex stood behind Shelly, put his arms over her shoulders, and hung on her neck from behind. Along with the other participants, they tried to walk around the room. She was asked how it felt to be dragging someone along behind her. Shelly replied, "This feels familiar in some ways. This is how I feel when I'm always trying to please Alex. But I think I'm more like the person hanging on the shoulders, because I'm really afraid that if I don't do what Alex wants, he'll leave me. My ex-husband used to tell me I was a weight around his neck. I bet this is how he felt."

Alex raised his hand and said, "I like to feel needed, so I was uncomfortable hanging on Shelly's back, but I know I could drag her around for hours. I feel important when I think someone needs me. But I don't want to end up supporting someone. I can see how that could happen if I let them depend on me too much." As the draggee, Alex is also dependent upon Shelly for his sense of importance, knowing she is "supporting" him. This is called codependence.

A codependent relationship results when one person does anything that prevents the other person from experiencing life and the consequences of it. A common name for this is "enabling." However, we use the term "discouraging" instead, to signify behaviors that sap courage and stop you or others from learning and growing from your mistakes. When Shelly dragged Alex around, it looked like the two were loving and close. But in fact, Shelly was doing all the work and stopping Alex from standing on his own two feet. Shelly could not thrive and grow, as most of her energy was going toward holding Alex up.

Like Shelly and Alex, you probably have been unaware of many of your discouraging behaviors. You may have thought this is how relationships are supposed to be. Is there an important relationship in which you are either a "dragger" or a "draggee"? Do dependent behaviors show up in your life?

To get a feel for what it's like to get out of a dependent relationship, picture yourself at the workshop with Shelly and Alex as the following activity unfolds. In this exercise, people lean back against their partner's outstretched hands, keeping their bodies straight, like an ironing board. The partners push them around the room in this position, saying, "I'm going to let go and I know you can stand on your own two feet." As soon as the "pushers" feel ready, they let go. When the pushers let go, to most people's surprise, no one falls down or leaves the room. In real life, most people never let go because they think someone will get hurt or abandon them. Not only does that not happen, but usually people end up feeling closer together. They see options that they didn't see before.

To illustrate an encouraging relationship, picture the following activity: Two people are standing facing each other about two feet apart. They notice how it feels to have some distance and to stand on their own two feet without anyone's support. They are both close enough together and apart enough that they can see all of themselves and each other. This stance symbolizes an **independent** relationship, where both people are able to stand on their own two feet. However, they are also available to help, cheer, or coach each other. Independent relationships are the first step toward interdependence. If you skip this step of independence, you won't attain interdependence.

Discover interdependent relationships

Now, to get the feel of an **interdependent** relationship, try the following activity. Stand a few feet apart from your partner. Each of you will rotate in your own circle, spinning slowly around to simulate your separate worlds. When either of you wants to make a connection, reach out with your hand, your eyes, or your words to invite the other to be closer for a time. When either of you wants more space, let the other know it's time to move back to your own revolving circle. Repeat this process of moving together and moving away, until you get the sense that doing your own thing doesn't mean you are abandoning each other. You will see that connection is possible at any time.

By simulating an interdependent relationship, you are practicing encouragement. Neither of you stands between the other person and his or her life. Both of you are available to help, mentor, and support each other. Interdependent relationships expand and never limit who you are.

Creating changes in your world

It's important to put what you are learning into practice, because whatever you practice, you'll get better at. You need to do your homework in the real world in order to create change. In *Do-It-Yourself Therapy*, taking small steps in the real world is an important and essential part of changing yourself.

It's amazing what you can do when you take one step. With any step you take, your view of the landscape changes. Each step you take increases your chances for success. If what you do doesn't work, you can try again, or do something else. Remember that mistakes are valuable when you view them as opportunities to learn.

We know that change will happen when you follow the suggestions offered here, even if they feel artificial and awkward at first. (Remember your interlaced fingers from page 24?) Eventually you'll look back and realize that what started out feeling uncomfortable has become a new behavior or skill that is part of you and that you have adapted to your own unique personality and style. It's important to remember that there is no finish line. Life is a process. It's how you live it, not what you achieve that makes for peace of mind, health, and happiness.

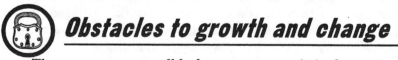

Obstacles to growth and change

There are many roadblocks you can unwittingly erect to make it tougher to change than it has to be. See if any of the following fit for you:

1. You may still be focusing on how someone else is creating problems for you or making your life miserable. Perhaps you're convinced that all your problems would be over, if only the other person would change. If you believe this, you keep victimizing yourself, denying the power of choice.
2. Maybe you think you or someone else is sick or defective in some way. Believing this makes growth or change impossible.

3. You may be stuck in the trap of believing, "I'm not good enough unless I change." Until you accept yourself and can say and believe, "I'm a valuable person and a worthwhile human being, in spite of my faults," change remains temporary if not impossible.

4. If you stop as soon you feel uncomfortable, instead of continuing to practice new ways of thinking and behaving until they are natural to you, you may be giving up when you're about to get the results you want.

5. Perhaps you're doing the same thing over and over, hoping each time for a different result. This is a severe energy drain that may leave you without the stamina to move forward.

6. Maybe like Don, you have a label you don't want to give up. It might be hard to imagine who you would be if you're no longer "The Pickiest Eater in the World."

7. If you're in a power struggle with someone, it would be hard to change if you thought you were giving in to somebody else or losing a battle.

8. Are you one of the countless people looking for that quick fix or a miracle cure? If it's not prescription drugs, maybe you're turning to television, marijuana, alcohol, food, or some other habit that you overuse until it becomes self-destructive.

9. Have you been practicing and reinforcing our recommendations for having a really bad day? These tips include: criticizing; judging or comparing yourself to others; thinking in concrete absolutes or creating catastrophes; practicing magical thinking or negative self-talk; thinking you have to be perfect; and blaming yourself for making mistakes, worrying about problems you don't have.

10. Does independence scare you? If you think you have to lean on others, or if you feel threatened as others grow and change around you, it's a good way to remain stuck. Or, if you feel like a nobody if someone isn't dependent on you, you should let go, freeing up energy that you need in order to grow.

11. Maybe your goals seem like impossible dreams. You may be thinking too far into the future. Or you may have unrealistic expectations about the change process.

Easy steps for change

Think about the relationship you want to work on this week and use the following list of ideas to help you get started. Put the list in a prominent place, and pick at least one suggestion to do each day. Try one thing at a time and keep working on it until you feel more comfortable.

☑ Ask other people how they think, feel, and do things, instead of trying to find the one "right" way to success.

☑ Know that if something isn't working, doing more of the same won't make the situation better. Try a different behavior.

☑ Ask for support and share with others. Don't think that you have to do everything by yourself.

☑ When practicing new behaviors, try them out first in the company of people with whom you feel safe.

☑ To learn new habits, set aside time for training. Make dates with a friend to strengthen your commitment to starting new routines. Get a calendar and write down what you will do.

☑ Pretend you have a magic wand to create pictures of how you might like your life to be. Then, behave as if it is already different. What would your behavior look like? Or, think about how you could behave in order to invite others to act the way you picture them.

☑ Don't give up easily. Think of making a change in terms of playing baseball: When you're tempted to stop at the hard part, imagine yourself running around all the bases instead of stopping at first base. If it's still too hard, get yourself a coach or cheerleader who will encourage you to stay on task.

☑ Get involved in therapy, educational programs, and recovery groups that offer drug-free approaches to growth and health. Show up and be open to people, places, and situations that are new to you. Allow yourself to experiment with different ways of thinking, feeling, and acting.

☑ Just do it. Sometimes, the best way to make a change is to stop thinking, talking, planning, and analyzing—just go for it. Decide on the first step you will take and do it. Learn what you need to do next from that step. The movement itself will give you feedback about what to do next.

Activities

Choose from the following activities for your first week of do-it-yourself therapy. We suggest doing several activities each week. You may wish to repeat the same activity at a later date because you may be in a different emotional state, or you may be working on a different relationship. Create a notebook for change. Use a journal, a folder, a spiral notebook, or even a napkin. Make sure to keep a record with dates, including the year, to help you track and acknowledge your progress. The notebook is only for you, although you may choose to share parts with people you trust. If you are seeing a therapist, bring your notebook with you to your sessions.

1.   Think about something that you have changed in your life and write about it. Then, read what you wrote and see if you can identify whether your change started by changing your thoughts, your feelings, or your actions. Notice how the change in one of those areas affected change in the others. Make notes for yourself about how you make changes, and what works best for you. Check back during the eight weeks to refresh your memory.

2.   Think about a relationship that you would like to improve. This could be a relationship with a child, a parent, a partner, a friend, or even with yourself. Write a letter to yourself about this relationship and answer the following questions. Why is this relationship important to you? If you had a magic wand, in what ways would you like it to be different? Are you already making changes in the relationship? Where are you in the change process? (Desire? Awareness? Acceptance? Options?)

3.   Go back to the experiment with the clasped hands on page 24. Think of a time when you felt awkward and uncomfortable about trying something new. What was it? What did you do? Do you still struggle with the problem or skill you were trying to learn? How did you encourage yourself to move forward, in spite of the discomfort? Write about this in your notebook.

4.   What are some of the labels you had as a child? How have these shaped your life? Have they helped you do better or

stopped you from moving forward? What would it mean to you to give up one of these labels? How do you imagine others around you would deal with the change? Write down your thoughts.

5. How do you feel about making mistakes? When you were a child, what happened if you made a mistake? How do you treat people around you when they make mistakes? How has it been changed by giving up? What do you think about the statement, "I know if I can't make it different on the 100th try, I need to experiment one more time, because the 101st time might be the charm?" How has your life been changed by trying again? Write down your answers.

6. Imagine yourself doing the experiences from the workshop on pages 31-33 with a person in a relationship you'd like to improve. You can increase your awareness of where you are on the "dependent, independent, interdependent" road map by doing these activities. You could gain a deeper understanding of the information by asking a friend to do these activities with you.

7. Remind yourself that life has cycles and that you may be in the down phase of a cycle. You might simply be in a "bad mood," or be having a "bad day (or two or three)." Knowing you won't always feel the way you do can keep a tough situation from getting worse.

8. You can increase your awareness of where you are on our "dependence, independence, interdependence" map by answering the questions on the "Dependency Checklist" on the next page. Think of a relationship that you would like to change or improve upon as you look at the following questions. Use a zero for always, a five for never, and the numbers in between for sometimes depending on the frequency, as you rank yourself on questions A-M.

If your total score for questions A through M is under 26, you have a healthy degree of independence and probably a fair amount of satisfaction in your life. With a score of 26-39, you are somewhat independent, but could gain significant individuation skills from our book. If your score is 40 or higher, you are highly dependent. You may see yourself as victimized, believe that you lack a sense of control over your life, and feel uncomfortable or unimportant. If this is so, this book will help you start "growing yourself up."

✓Dependency Checklist

When filling in this checklist, use 0 for always, 5 for never, and 1-4 for sometimes.

A. Do you refrain from giving or taking orders from others?

_____

B. Do you allow for separateness from your significant others? Separate time, separate interests, separate friends?

_____

C. Do you believe that other people's happiness is up to them?

_____

D. Do you say what's on your mind even when it may upset someone else?

_____

E. Do you say no to another person when you want to?   _____

F. Do you rely on alcohol or drugs (including prescription drugs) to make you feel better?

_____

*If you are already or were suddenly on your own,
could you deal with the following:*

G. Keeping commitments, promises, appointments?   _____

H. Maintaining your living quarters, including those things that need to be done on a daily basis to support and take care of your household?

_____

I. Maintaining the outside of your living quarters? This includes all those things that need to be done to support and take care of your environment.

_____

J. Finding and holding a job?   _____

K. Your laundry, clothing, and food needs?   _____

L. Your transportation?   _____

M. Your finances?   _____

Week 2

Find the Card You Play to Resist Change

D o you ever feel that you want to change and yet are afraid to change at the same time? Change can be both exciting and frightening, so you use a method to cope with your stress and fears about changing. There are four distinct styles that people use to cope. We call these protective styles "top cards." Top card information is based on our study of Adlerian ideas that have been around for years and are called "personality priorities" or "number-one priorities" by most Adlerians.

This week, you'll discover what your top card is, how you learned to play it, and what happens when you do. You'll learn how to use this top card information to help you face your fears so you can move forward with greater ease.

Every person has two basic needs: belonging and significance. Belonging means feeling connected, accepted, and part of a greater whole. Significance refers to how you are unique, distinct, and special. As long as you feel a sense of belonging and significance, you act in ways that meet the needs of the situation and contribute to your well-being and to the well-being of others. But, when you think your belonging and significance are threatened, you feel stressed and react instinctively to protect yourself.

The diagram on the next page shows you a different way of looking at this. The top line in the diagram represents how you think life should be, while the bottom line is the way things really are. The distance between these two lines represents stress, and the larger the space, the greater your stress.

The way life should be

STRESS

The way life really is

Your top card behavior is what you do first and what other people see first when you feel afraid, threatened, or stressed. You move into a protective style of behavior that is aimed at keeping your belonging and significance intact. There are four "protective styles, and the one you spontaneously slip into is what we call your top card. The moment you do that, you set yourself up to receive exactly which you are trying to avoid.

How to discover your top card

First, you need to determine which of the four protective styles is yours. Keep in mind, no top card is better or worse than another. Top cards are neither good nor bad. Rather, they are simply part of what each of us does. They can take us either to the useful or the useless side of life, depending on what we do with them. (*See* Week 6 for more information about the useful vs. the useless sides of life.) The four protective styles are called: Comfort (or Avoidance), Control, Pleasing, and Superiority.

To identify which top card is yours, imagine you've just been handed the four packages shown on the next page. Even though you might not want any of the contents, you can refuse only one. Which one has the

 Hint   Top cards: friend or foe?

Some people find top card the most helpful part of do-it-yourself therapy. Other people are put off at first and discover the usefulness later. No one can grasp all of the information in one reading, so don't worry if it seems confusing. We suggest that you read Weeks Two and Three, both of which focus on top card, with a "go-easy-on-yourself attitude," picking and choosing the parts that fit and are most useful for you. Some of you may discover what your top card is, and that will be all you want and need to know for now; others may enjoy implementing many features of top card. Either way, you'll want to review the top card chapters frequently.

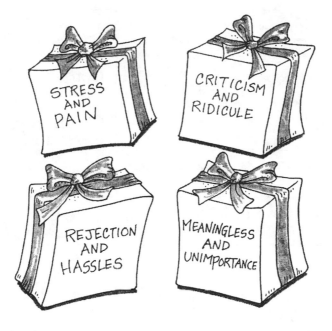

contents that are most objectionable to you? Read aloud what is in each of the packages and check yourself to see if you have a physical reaction to any items as you read them (such as a tightening or tenseness in your body, flush, heat flash, tingling, going blank, and so forth). If so, that's a good indication that you've identified your top card. Choose the box you'd like the least and then look at the chart on the next page to find out your top card. If you aren't certain which package you would refuse, the information in the middle column may help you decide which top card is your best fit.

There is yet another way to discover your top card. If you think this whole exercise is pointless, your top card is most likely Superiority. If you want to make sure you've understood all the details before you choose so that you don't make a mistake, or if you would prefer no one knows what your top card is, it's probably Control. If you want to completely avoid choosing or are about to flip to another section in the book, it's likely your top card is Comfort. But if you think this is the most fabulous information you've come across in years and can't wait to learn how to use it, you must have a Pleasing top card.

If your top card is Comfort/Avoidance, you seek a comfort zone by avoiding having to deal with situations. If your top card is Control, you try to control your feelings, situations, or people. If you have a Pleasing top card, you try to figure out what will please others in order to provide what they want. Finally, if your top card is Superiority, you try

If you chose to refuse the box with	You probably often experience	And your top card is called
Stress and pain	Boredom or lack of productivity	Comfort (like the turtle)
Criticism and ridicule	Lack of intimacy or spontaneity	Control (like the eagle)
Rejection and hassles	Not knowing who you are, hurt feelings	Pleasing (like the chameleon)
Meaninglessness and unimportance	Exhaustion, feeling disliked by others	Superiority (like the lion)

to accomplish something truly superior or make things perfect to find meaning and importance, or you attempt to get others to see or do what you think is important.

The chart on the facing page describes more of the top card behaviors and is another resource to help you select your top card. Not everything in "your" column may fit for you because we're all individuals. Some of these behaviors may be more problematic than others. Notice which descriptions you do recognize. It's only natural that all the cards seem to fit to some degree because you have aspects of them all in your personality, but your *top card is what you do first, unconsciously, and automatically when you feel threatened.* Each top card has challenges as well as distinct assets, and depending on the situation, any behavior can make your life work better or it can create problems for you. It's a good idea to avoid labeling behaviors as positive or negative. For instance, if you play a Pleasing top card, you have the ability to socialize, laugh, make jokes, and cheer others on. This is certainly an asset in some circumstances, but can be a liability when your behavior doesn't match your true feelings.

How you learned to play your top card

Spend some time watching babies and young children. Notice how they watch what is going on around them, try out things, and then see what kind of responses they get. Since they have very little life experience and no spoken language skills, their conclusions or "decisions" about

Top card behaviors

Comfort (Avoidance)	Control	Pleasing	Superiority
Make jokes, intellectualize, or bite someone's head off. Do only the things you already do well. Avoid new experiences. Take the path of least resistance. Leave sentences incomplete. Avoid taking a risk. Hide so no one can discover that you aren't perfect. Make things harder than they look. Figure out ways to avoid doing what you don't want to do. Wait until you are ready, no matter how much others push. Block your feelings. Avoid discussing topics that make you uncomfortable. Act as if a conflict never happened. You do what you do well and you're easy going. You make others feel comfortable. People like being around you.	Hold back. Boss others. Organize. Argue. Get quiet and wait for others to coax you. Do it yourself. Stuff your feelings. Cover all the bases before you make a move. Give instructions whether asked to or not. Wait too long and lose out on opportunities. Refuse to be pushed or participate if you don't have a choice. Prioritize and plan ahead to the point of loss of spontaneity. Try to fix things for others. Act as a crisis manager. Have lots of rules. Restrict the use of your things. You're assertive and persistent and well-organized. You are law-abiding and get what you want. You can get things done. You have endless patience. You're a good leader but a poor delegator.	Act friendly. Say yes and mean no. Give in. Worry about what others want. Give over and completely lose yourself. Gossip instead of confronting directly. Try to fix everything and make everybody happy. Let others decide if it seems important to them. Secretly undermine their plans when you're not pleased. Let others go first. Socialize, laugh, joke, and cheer others on. Don't say what you really want, think, or feel. You're sensitive to others, have lots of friends, and are a good compromiser. Sacrifice yourself instead of asking others. You volunteer often and people know they can count on you. You see the positives in people and things and are very optimistic.	Set people straight. Give others advice which to them may seem like a put-down. Overdo and try to plan every detail to avoid failure. Take on too much. Worry about always doing better. Think in black and white. Make things bigger than they are. Blame yourself when things don't work out. Feel responsible for everything. Spend time, energy, and money to get the best equipment. Get frustrated when everyone doesn't listen to your ideas. Do anything to avoid inefficiency. You may be overwhelming and too intense for others. You are loyal and reliable, except when discouraged or when dealing with something you don't think is important.

themselves, others, and the world are based on feelings, gestures, sounds, and so forth. If they feel uncomfortable or threatened, they unintentionally and unconsciously create coping behaviors.

For example, one child may hide behind a parent's leg to avoid trying something new (Comfort/Avoidance). Another might feel humiliated when scolded for some behavior, retreating to his or her room to avoid future criticism (Control). A third child might try to be charming and cute to make others smile instead of frown (Pleasing). A fourth could cry in frustration when he colors outside the lines and refuse to continue (Superiority).

Like these children, you also created a collection of coping behaviors before you were five years old. You may have observed others playing out these behaviors and mimicked them. Or, through trial and error, you may have perfected behaviors that you thought protected you from not belonging or from feeling insignificant. Every time you felt threatened, you practiced these protective moves which we call "playing your top card."

If Comfort is your top card, you may have believed that if things were too stressful or too painful or too hard, you weren't up to the task(s) at hand and couldn't possibly belong and be significant. If Control is your top card and you were certain someone criticized you, you felt humiliated at the possibility that you weren't as good as you thought you were, and therefore, couldn't possibly belong or have significance. If your top card is Pleasing, maybe you were sure you lost belonging and significance when others weren't happy with you or with your behavior, or when you thought others rejected you. And if your top card is Superiority, you probably thought that if you weren't important or life wasn't meaningful, you no longer had significance or belonged. Whatever you practiced, you became skilled at, and today, you use these behaviors automatically in response to stress, fear, or perceived threats.

(!) Hint   A top card is what you do, not who you are

A common mistake when learning about top card is to say, "I am a Superiority top card," or "He is a Control top card." Even though people with the same top cards might have a lot in common with each other, your top card doesn't describe *who you are* or *what you want*, but rather is about *what you do* when you are scared or stressed. Describing your top card might sound like this, "My way of playing my Superiority top card is to complain about the people that I work with."

Face your fears

The more skills you have, the better your life works. Yet when you play your top card, you limit your learning of new skills. You have fewer resources to draw upon and life becomes more stressful. Your top card works against you when you play it without awareness or understanding. When you play your top card instead of facing your fear, you end up being stuck experiencing exactly what you are trying to avoid, as shown inside the boxes on page 41.

Once you learn to recognize what your coping behaviors are, you can catch yourself in the act. You can also ask other people this question when you see them playing their top cards. Once you understand your fears, you will be able to face it and see your options clearly.

Ask yourself what is the worst thing that could happen if what you fear came to pass, and whether you could deal with that. To track down your fear, keep asking yourself, "What am I afraid of? What about that bothers me? And what about that would bother me? And what about that?" As you dig deeper, your answer to "What about that would bother me?" will keep coming back to the same issue. This will relate to one or more of four basic human needs: recognition, power, justice, and skills.

Finding your underlying issues

Recognition is your need to be acknowledged and appreciated for who you are. It's also about wanting others to treat you like you're special, to make life easier for you, or to show their love. It's about having others notice, include, and involve you. If you discovered that your recognition needs aren't being met, here's how you can work with your fear: Remind yourself of all the things about you that are unique and special. Don't be afraid to ask someone for extra attention or help, even if it seems embarrassing or silly. If you can't think of anything special about yourself, ask a friend to help you out.

Power is your need for a sense of control and choices. You want to do what you want and still belong, and not be bossed around. Power is about being capable and having an opportunity to help. And it's about having and showing your feelings without ending up in an emotional eruption. If any of this is what's under your "fear pile," you know your need for power isn't being met, and here's how you can work with your fear. Look for ways to put more positive power in your life. You can be powerful without having power over others. Decide what you want and what is important to you. Be assertive about your needs and preferences. If you think others aren't giving you choices, say, "I need some choices here so I don't feel bossed around." If you feel angry, say, "I'm angry," and then follow it up by stating clearly what you want or wish would happen.

Justice is your need for fairness. It's your need to know you count as much as everyone else, and that others will treat you that way. Justice is about your wish to feel good when others do, and for others to feel bad when you do. If after all your "What is it about this that bothers me?" questions, you keep coming to how you're not cared about, or that others have it better, or that things aren't fair and you have hurt feelings, your fear revolves around issues of justice. You can work with your fear— remind yourself that everyone has a different idea about what is fair. If you think things aren't fair, tell others what you think and why, and ask for their ideas. Don't be afraid to tell someone you are feeling hurt and that you suspect they might be feeling the same way.

Skills have to do with your need to feel competent and able. Skills are also about wanting to keep up with others or to be as good as they are, to be good enough at doing whatever needs to be done. You need to feel that neither you nor others will give up on you even if you struggle with something. Yet, when you're discouraged, you may be thinking that unless you are perfect, or already know how to do everything, you have failed and should give up trying. If under your "What is my fear?" pile, you find these kinds of concerns and issues, here's how you can work with your fear: Notice when you are stopping yourself if you don't think you can do something or your results aren't good enough. Remember that we are all beginners at one time or another and taking those small steps is the way to build skills. It's okay to ask others not to give up on you.

Eric's story

Eric discovered his top card must be Control because he cringed involuntarily when he read the words "criticism" and "humiliation" inside the box. He felt himself flush as he recognized many of the behaviors in the "Control" column of the chart on page 43, but what most caught his attention was, "Give instructions and information whether asked to or not." He remembered a recent phone conversation with his daughter, who was attending her first year of college away from home. In that conversation, he was telling Lonnie when, where, and how to register, and which classes she should consider. Lonnie was edgy and dismissive of Eric's suggestions, telling him not to keep trying to parent long-distance and that she could run her own life just fine. "What am I afraid of?" he wondered. He began asking himself the "What about that..." questions, and his mental conversation went like this:

What am I afraid of?
She'll overlook some detail in the registration procedure and miss her chance to get the best possible schedule.

What about that would bother me?
She'll end up wasting time taking classes that don't fulfill her requirements and she'll take longer to graduate.

And what about that would bother me?
I'll have to listen to and know about her pain when she discovers she's run out of money and can't finish school without getting a job.

And what about that would bother me?
I won't have enough money to help her or I won't want to spend money I have because she could have avoided this if she had paid attention.

And what about that?
I could have prevented her from making a mistake but she wouldn't let me.

And what about that?
If she'd done it my way, this wouldn't have happened.

Eric realized his underlying issue was about power. His fears might come true if she didn't let him help with information and instructions. He was trying to prevent problems from happening ahead of time so he wouldn't find himself powerless to help later if Lonnie made mistakes. When he asked himself if he could handle that, should it come to pass, the answer was decidedly yes—he just didn't want to.

In their next conversation, Eric told Lonnie, "If your schedule or something else isn't working out the way you want, or you're feeling overwhelmed and confused, it would really help me if you would talk to your roommate, a department person, or someone else to get some ideas about what you're going to do. Then give me a call. I won't feel so on the spot to help you figure out what to do when I don't have a clue." Lonnie's response was practical. "If that's all it takes to keep you from micro-managing my freshman year, it's fine with me!"

Your top card vs. your everyday style

You may feel confused because your normal behavior looks more like some other top card in the chart on page 42. This is because you could have an everyday style that is different from your top card.

Playing your top card is what you do automatically, when you feel threatened. Your everyday style, on the other hand, is how you operate the rest of the time when you're not stressed. It isn't unusual to have an everyday style that is different from your top card. If you had a strong second choice when you identified the box that contained the items you most wanted to avoid, you may have already discovered your everyday style. If you aren't sure what your everyday style is, go back to the chart on page 43 and review it to help you find which collection of behaviors seems to fit your everyday style.

In the next chapter, we'll look more closely at everyday styles, as well as how different top cards interact. For now, keep in mind that if people are engaging in some of the behaviors from the chart that are causing problems, they are afraid and trying to protect themselves. Instead of reacting to their behavior, you can find out about their fear by saying, "You're playing your top card right now, so I'm guessing you feel threatened or are afraid of something. Do you know what that might be?" If you're curious, you can take a sneak peak at a chart of everyday styles in Week 3, but we suggest that you spend this week understanding your top card.

Which animal are you?

Associating each top card with its respective animal will help you understand the information better. Look at the charts on pages 42 and 43 to see which animal best characterizes your coping behaviors when you are stressed, afraid, or threatened. (Our colleague, Steve Cunningham, introduced us to the animals, and we are grateful for his humor and clarity.) The following sections cover all four top cards.

We asked people with each top card what helped them make changes and we have shared the information here. You will probably want to start by focusing on your particular top card to learn more about yourself, paying special attention to how you can improve or empower yourself. Bear in mind that everything we've written about people with your top card may not be true of you. However, by identifying what does fit, you'll learn to recognize what your personal version of that coping style looks like. Eventually, we hope you will read about all the top cards so you can understand and deal with others more effectively.

Turtles: people with Comfort top card

If you play a Comfort top card, you have much in common with the turtle. A turtle likes to move at its own pace. It is always at home inside its rock hard-shell, safe from enemies. When threatened, it pulls in and stays there, or it snaps to protect itself. Turtles have endured for centuries without changing, spending the day lying in the sun or swimming lazily. "Slow but steady wins the race" describes the turtle's ability to take care of what's needed in a way that isn't stressful. The turtle is able to finish the race without being sidetracked. Does this sound familiar?

Joanie's story

Joanie plays a Comfort/Avoidance top card when she feels threatened. She supports someone else's opinion even when she doesn't agree rather than being put on the spot. She loves it when someone else does all the talking, even though she is usually talking a mile a minute in her head. There's nothing wrong with what Joanie thinks, but she draws in, hides and screens herself to avoid attracting anyone's scrutiny, just in case she might be wrong. We find many people with Comfort/Avoidance top cards comparing themselves to others who are farther along and deciding that they couldn't possibly do as well or as perfectly, and like Joanie, they retreat to their comfort zone rather than trying out something new.

Joanie is fairly predictable, self-sufficient, independent, steady, peaceful, and gentle. She makes few demands on others to help her. She's easygoing and looks out for herself and her needs. Like the turtle with its house on its back, Joanie has the ability to make sure she has the comforts of home with her wherever she goes. She likes to help others feel comfortable as long as they don't move outside of her comfort zone. If others try to pull Joanie out of her shell, she acts like a snapping turtle and bites their heads off in an effort to get them to stay back where she feels safe.

People think Joanie is lazy or pessimistic, especially when they don't realize how scared she is. When Joanie looks at the rose bush, she usually notices the thorns. Joanie plays her Comfort top card by rescuing, reminding, sidetracking, or protecting others in an attempt to make everyone comfortable. As a result she ends up with people who expect her to fulfill their needs and do things for them that they could easily do for themselves. This tendency to indulge others creates just what she is trying to avoid: extreme stress and pain. Joanie ends up by complaining about not accomplishing anything and feeling bored with herself and her life.

New and improved turtles

When you catch yourself playing your Comfort/Avoidance top card like Joanie, you can begin to expect others to handle their own affairs, even though this may be uncomfortable for you at first. Your best therapy is to continue to remind yourself that you are capable of learning new things with a step-by-step approach. Have faith in your ability to get started.

You benefit greatly when you insist that others let you go at your own pace or do things your way. It makes your day when people have faith in you. You can move forward with ease when others encourage you to take small steps toward your goals. It's a gift when others are curious about what you have to say instead of assuming they know what you mean when you don't finish your sentences. You love it when someone reciprocates—providing you with comforts and doing special things for you.

It's all right to ask people for help. In fact, it's empowering and encouraging to you and to them when you let others know exactly what you need. You'll be surprised how others will help when they know what works best for your top card. Don't hesitate to tell someone if you are feeling stress or pain. If you can, tell them the ways they can either step back, or ways they can support you and encourage you to feel capable.

After working with top card information for several months, Joanie said, "When I catch myself playing my top card, I remind myself that there is something I fear, and I try to figure out what that is. I do that by asking myself, 'What is the worst thing that could happen?' When I know what the worst thing is, I think about whether I could handle it. If I believe I can handle the worst, I can move forward and face my fear, taking one step at a time. When I work on my fears before an issue gets more intense or complicated, I feel better, and so do the people around me."

Eagles: people with Control top cards

If you most want to avoid criticism and ridicule, then your top card is Control, which we feel is best exemplified by the eagle. With their sharp claws, hooked beaks, and huge wing span, eagles look powerful and strong. However, they are not as fierce as they seem. Eagles nest in inaccessible places and keep to themselves, protected by distance. When eagles seek refuge by flying away to their nests, others don't have a chance to make contact and have to wait for them to come down. Flying high, eagles can see the lay of the land before they make a move, and not much gets past their sharp "eagle eyes." Is any of this true for you?

Howie's story

When Howie plays his Control top card, he tries to be on top of every situation so he doesn't end up being criticized or ridiculed.

Although he is extremely organized, making checklists of things to do each day, he often procrastinates when things feel too overwhelming to control. Often, he sits in front of the television, instead of attacking his many piles of "to-do" items. He feels most uncomfortable when things are thrown at him or when someone expects him to perform on command without allowing him time to think and prepare. He hates being told how to do things, because that implies that he's incompetent. When he is asked about something he doesn't know, he feels caught and humiliated.

Howie is very involved on a board of directors for a local organization. He is able to take charge of situations, figure things out, get jobs accomplished, and usually get what he wants. Even though he prefers to plan ahead, he can be a real asset in a crisis because he jumps right in, managing things assertively and competently. He also has an uncanny ability to wait patiently if necessary to get what he wants.

At the same time, some of his fellow board members complain that Howie is bossy, defensive, arrogant, and inflexible. In his efforts to prevent others from finding his weak spots, he is sometimes perceived as distant and remote or as controlling, lacking any spontaneity. He has a need to get permission before he takes control of a situation, and sometimes that permission never comes.

We find that people who play out eagle-like behaviors tend to have an authoritarian style, trying to control others' behavior and lives in order to keep things under control. Like Howie, they prefer doing things themselves and have a hard time delegating because they don't trust others to do things the right way. When Howie acts this way, he invites rebellion and resistance, which then leads to power struggles.

Howie's tendency to hold back and not share his innermost thoughts and feelings results in a lack of intimacy. He finds it difficult to have satisfactory relationships because of his fear of sharing information or speaking his truths. Few people have ever seen an eagle "up close and personal." If Howie and other eagle types handle conflict by getting quiet, flying away, or holding their emotions in, they often end up with stress in their bodies, which comes out in the form of physical symptoms and illnesses. (*See* Week 7 for more on mind/body connection.)

New and improved eagles

If Control is your top card, like Howie, you need to tell others what's going on with you, how you're feeling, and what you're thinking. As fearful as you may be about being exposed or losing control, sharing your true feelings and saying what you want is the best therapy for someone with a Control top card. There's a difference between sharing feelings and dumping them on others, so be respectful when you tell others how you feel. If you've been acting defensively, try saying, "I'm feeling criticized by you. I'm not saying you mean to criticize me, but I'm having a hard time proceeding when I feel this upset."

After reading about his top card, Howie realized he needed to take a risk and ask people for their help. He wanted them to feel involved, and have time for his other interests. He decided to start with his work on the board of a nonprofit organization he belonged to. Since he liked working from a checklist, he wrote down all the tasks he was currently responsible for. He was shocked to see how many there were. At the next board meeting, Howie asked his fellow members for help with some of the items on his ever increasing "to-do" list. They were happy to help out, because they had been very uncomfortable noticing his workload. Howie wanted to continue to sort things out before each meeting and then identify items he could delegate.

Howie eventually noticed that board members had started appreciating what he did. After one of the meetings, Howie explained to a friend how he had changed, "I started realizing I had this automatic response to any need—I'd do everything myself. I figured there had to be other ways to handle some of what came up. I still feel some discomfort about delegating responsibilities. But I'm not giving in to my desire to control everything, because it's obvious by now how that backfires for me."

Chameleons: people with Pleasing top cards

If your top card is Pleasing, consider the chameleon carefully to better understand your stressed behavior. Sensitive to environmental factors, such as light, temperature, or emotions (especially fright), a chameleon's first line of defense is to undergo a wide range of color changes in order to blend into the scenery. If the threat continues, the chameleon charges and snaps its jaws. If still threatened, the chameleon moves into a crevice and puffs up so it can't be removed. If attacked, some chameleons can leave their tails behind, scurrying to safety. Later, their tails grow back again. Chameleons are carefully observant—each eye moves independently, enabling them to watch all that's going on around them. Does this sound like you?

Priscilla's story

Priscilla, the "queen of chameleons," plays her Pleasing card continually to avoid rejection and hassles. She's seen as someone who's friendly, flexible, and considerate. The last thing she wants is to behave in any way that would make someone mad or not like her.

Priscilla runs a one-person graphic design company where she worries more about what others want than she does about her own needs. She'll do anything to look good and keep out of trouble. She doesn't always do what she promises because she is so overcommitted that she can't possibly meet all of her deadlines. Priscilla can drive her customers crazy, because they want her to use her talents and knowledge to give ideas and choices, and not wait for their opinions.

On the other hand, one of Priscilla's assets is her extreme sensitivity to those around her. She has many customers and friends. She's not threatening, and she's very accommodating and adaptable in her work. Because she can read others so well, she is able to come up with designs her customers love. They constantly remark that Priscilla sees the best in them and reflects their personalities in her logos and designs. However, that same sensitivity can cause Priscilla pain when she becomes overly sensitive. She is easily crushed because she takes everything personally.

Priscilla can drive others crazy with her indecisiveness and chameleon-like changeability. She gives in much of the time, and then feels resentful when others don't accommodate her in turn. Instead of speaking up, she finds it easier to talk behind someone's back or react in anger. People around her may pick up her change in energy, but they must guess what is going on or must try to coax Priscilla to tell them, because she will say everything is fine, even when it's not. Others are then unsure of what is really going on, and are therefore at a loss to make it better.

New and improved chameleons

Like Priscilla and other chameleons, you will experience less rejection if they have faith in others to work out their own problems. You can avoid most problems by practicing emotional honesty. This means saying how you feel and what you need. Say this directly to the person with whom you are having difficulties, and as quickly as possible.

Priscilla finds it extremely helpful when she knows others approve of her and love her. Sometimes she has to ask for reassurance that she can say what she is really feeling, or do what she really wants to do. When Priscilla told her friends and customers she wanted them to think of her as cute and adorable even when she was being obnoxious, they laughed. One of them said, "Priscilla, we know you are a character and we love you. You provide us with constant entertainment, even when you are annoying." This can be very reassuring for Priscilla and other chameleons, but they also want to know that if you are upset with them, you'll stick around and work things out without being mad, punishing, or attacking.

Priscilla worked to make changes by confronting people directly, instead of complaining about them behind their backs. She also worked on her courage to ask questions, instead of assuming that every problem was about her.

When she felt overwhelmed and hassled, Priscilla began to ask for the help she needed, instead of pouting, thinking that others were selfish for not helping out. It's a great gift when others can make life easier for chameleons, but it's important to check first whether the chameleon wants the help. Priscilla realized that she'd been redoing the work of others who didn't intuit how she wanted things done. Until she learned about her top card, she had been doing extra work rather than risk what had seemed to her to be an impossible confrontation.

Chameleons can be very picky and like things a certain way—their way. This seems contrary to their desire to please, but they are hypersensitive to change. When the need to please one's self is stronger than the need to please others, the chameleon-minded person ends up being picky to relieve their tension. They need to learn how to tell others what bothers them, instead of acting indirectly.

Priscilla felt even more encouraged when she realized that she could be more accepting of herself, too. "It helps to tell myself, this is how I am. I am a picky person and I probably won't change, and that's okay."

Lions: people with Superiority top cards

If your top card is Superiority, picturing your temperament as a lion's will give you a picture of how you cope under stress. The qualities that lions possess are contradictory. When angry or hungry, lions will charge with great speed and ferocity. But at other times, they will lie around and sleep all day. They often roar loudly, but can just as easily purr like giant pussycats. Lions work together to hunt prey, but they also hunt alone by pouncing on their targets. Humans tend to view lions as the king of the jungle—proud, cunning, and strong—or as a caged animal in a zoo. Which one of these qualities describes you?

Pablo's story

Pablo dealt himself a Superiority top card and he doesn't waste his time doing anything that's not important. He avoids situations where his imperfections show. His mother constantly points out how he fails to follow through on his promises to help around the house. So instead, Pablo avoids her and prefers to spend time doing what is important to him. He knows he can be number one lifting weights at the health club, or as the kids' favorite coach on the soccer field.

Pablo, like others with Superiority top cards, sees situations in extremes. Like the mighty lion, people with Superiority top cards will never stand up to an opponent, whether he or she be a parent, spouse, significant other, boss, or customer.

Pablo appears to be very self-assured, and in those activities that matter to him, he is a model of competence, success, and initiative, even if he has to spend every waking moment perfecting himself. He has high standards and expectations for both himself and others. His intensity and passion show when he is involved in something he believes to be important. He can be counted on to work hard to accomplish a goal. For example, he will spend hours reading magazines and training manuals on body building, soccer strategy, and coaching.

Like the lion, Pablo and others with Superiority top cards embody extremes. For all his productivity and standards of excellence, he's frequently dissatisfied, thinking he should have done a better job. He often feels overwhelmed and overburdened and takes on too much. Sometimes, he finds it difficult even to get out of bed because no matter how much he's done, it never feels like enough.

At this point, the "shoulds" begin to run his life: He *should* have played professional soccer. He *should* have gone to college and gotten an advanced degree in exercise physiology. He *should* be making more money. He *should* move out of his mother's house. Then, he admonishes himself for worrying about this, because it sounds so materialistic. When his mother asks whether he's making progress finding a job and looking for a place of his own, he roars like a lion in anger, instead of solving his dilemmas.

Pablo is perceived by others as knowledgeable in soccer and weightlifting. Although he's generous with his knowledge, it can be difficult for him to put up with the imperfections around him. In his attempt to help others by "setting them straight," he often comes across as a critical know-it-all, leaving others feeling inadequate.

New and improved lions

If you have a Superiority top card and lion-like behaviors, it is important to let go of the belief that you have the one right way. There are different ways of looking at and doing things. For example, holding

family meetings and group conferences where everyone has an opportunity to share ideas offers a forum where all ideas are valued and
shared. We recommend you start these immediately. Make sure that
at your meetings you ask for information from others first, instead of
telling them what you think. Recognize that you have a difficult time
with empathy and that you have to work hard at listening to what
others think. As you realize that what others have to say is their opinion and not an order, this attitude opens useful dialogue to help you
come up with win/win solutions to difficulties.

After learning about his top card, Pablo decided he wanted to lighten
up and stop being so serious and worried about perfection. He wanted
to work on creating balance in his life. When Pablo said he might be
interested in becoming a personal trainer, his mother asked him if he'd
like some help in researching the field. He thanked her for her concern
and said he could do that on his own, and he did. He loved it when his
mother commented on his drive, intensity, and ability to focus. If you
practice lion-like behaviors, and you don't get the appreciation you need,
it's perfectly all right to ask for it. It's also helpful to let people know
that you do your best when something is important to you and that you
have a hard time doing what seems meaningless.

When Pablo sensed others were judging him or disliked him, he
realized he could *check it out*. Checking things out released a lot of the
pressure Pablo carried. He said, "When I notice I really clash with someone, I try to find out what their top card is and adjust my response accordingly. Instead of looking down at them with disdain, I am curious
about how they view things, and I ask them to tell me more about how
they see them."

 ## *Creating changes in your world*

The information in this chapter could change your life. For many of
our clients, it has been the key that opened the door to self-acceptance
and to understanding others. The majority of our clients say that learning about their top card accelerated change more dramatically than anything else they learned in therapy, because it provided them with an
immediate way to feel understood, along with a simple map for creating
more respectful relationships.

One of our clients commented on how the knowledge of her top
card changed her life. As you read her story, you will see that working
with top card information was a process for her.

"When I first heard about top card and realized mine was Control, I wanted to crawl under my chair. I didn't have a single doubt that the word fit me. I could recognize the strengths that went with it, and that felt good. But the liabilities were all big issues for me at the time. Seeing that, I felt sad.

"My top card was running my life everyday and I was constricted by it. Slowly over time, I recognized how fear-based I was as I moved through the world. Just realizing that increased my compassion for other people who I noticed playing their top cards. I knew they were in pain and dealing with it in counterproductive ways. It helped me a lot to know that everyone has some form of discouragement and that nobody is perfect. I could take a new look at my perfectionism and obsessive compulsive tendencies and rituals and realize it wasn't that I was a flawed person, I was simply playing my top card.

"When I felt more encouraged, I was able to ask my husband and children to give me a signal when they caught me playing my control card. Instead of hearing what they said as criticism, I was able to hear it as help, as well as a reminder that I had choices when facing my fears. Knowing about my top card was a relief, because I realized everyone had one and I wasn't bad. It was normal to use a coping mechanism

Hint   The best therapy for:

Comfort/Avoidance
☑ Continue to remind yourself that you are capable of learning new things with a step-by-step approach.
☑ Have faith in yourself to get started.

Control
☑ Share your true feelings and say what you want.

Pleasing
☑ Practice emotional honesty.
☑ Say how you feel and what you need.
☑ Say this directly to the person with whom you are having difficulties, and as quickly as possible.

Superiority
☑ Let go of the belief that you have **the** one right way.

when faced with stress. I didn't have to take everything personally when other people were offended or offensive with me. They just might be playing their own top cards."

Using the information in the **Obstacles to Growth and Change**, **Easy Steps for Change**, and **Activities** sections that follow will help you work this week on using top card to change your life in the real world.

Obstacles to growth and change

As you go through the information in the chapter and try things out during the week, look for these obstacles. These will slow down the change process and make it harder for you to contribute positively to your well-being and the well-being of others.

1. If you use the top card to label who you are instead of what you do, you could be creating problems instead of expanding your awareness and improving relationships.

2. If you spend too much time trying to figure out the difference between your top card and your everyday style, you'll be creating more stress and less learning, caught up in overanalyzing.

3. If you worry too much about whether you chose the right top card, you will miss out on the value this information has for you.

4. You might decide to skip through this information because it seems overwhelming.

5. You could forget that playing your top card results in getting what you are trying to avoid.

6. You could neglect to ask yourself, "What is my fear? What is the worst thing that could happen? Could I deal with it?"

7. You might take other people's misbehavior personally instead of realizing that they are responding from fear and playing their top card.

Easy steps for change

Put the following list of choices somewhere you can easily refer to it. Once a day, pick one of the items to use.

☑ Identify your top card. Go with your first choice.

☑ Get together with your friends to discover everyone's top card.

☑ Ask others to let you know when they see you playing your top card.

☑ Talk to others and ask them how they play their top cards. See how it affects their lives.

☑ Think about your top card animal and the characteristics you have in common with it.

☑ Remind yourself that your top card isn't good or bad, but that awareness of it can help you.

☑ Reread sections in this chapter to help clarify the information. Use the top card chart to look for behaviors that you possess. Circle them.

☑ Make copies of the charts in the chapter and carry them with you as a reference or post them on the refrigerator.

☑ Keep a journal of the times you are most likely to play your top card as well as times you did play it. Review the material in this chapter.

☑ Each time you play your top card, look for your underlying fear issue, read the section on how to work with your fear and try out some of the suggestions.

Activities

Top cards provide opportunities for some playful and fun-filled activities. You don't have to suffer to learn. Participants in our workshops have shown us time and time again how using humor and exaggeration help point out the foibles of their top cards. Although some of the information may seem negative, most participants will tell us that they *like* the way they play their top cards. Any of these activities will help you to gain insight about yourself and others. We recommend doing all of them. They are easy and enjoyable.

1. Look at the chart on page 60. It lists various top card bumper stickers and mottoes that participants at workshops have made up. Circle the ones that fit for you. See if you can add any to the list.

2. If you were writing an ad for the personals, what would it sound like? Pretend you are writing your ad to reflect your top card. Feel free to use ideas from the samples provided.

Top card bumper stickers			
Comfort	Control	Pleasing	Superiority
Forget the gain, no pain!	We've got the answer.	We aim to please.	I do more in an hour than you do all day.
Do less...less stress.	I need your help? Not!	Tell me what you want.	Nobody does it better.
Get off my tail!	I've got it under control.	Your pleasure is my pleasure.	I'd rather be right than happy.
If it isn't broken...	Follow me, I'm in control.	We don't stand for anything.	We're #1.
We avoid everything.	I break for crises.	I know what will make you happy.	It's been a long day so get to the point.
Don't worry, be happy.	My way or no way.	We have what you want.	We bring only good things to life.
Turtle crossing.	Feelings? What feelings?	Have a nice day!	Question authority.
What, me worry?	Keep your distance.	Smile!	I was wrong once but I was mistaken.
Let it be.	Born to be in control.	No offense.	Too bad you're not in our group.
Go with the flow.	Don't worry. I'll do it.	When you really need yes, turn to us.	We know it all!
Slow and steady wins the race.	Cover all the bases.	Peace!	If you want it done right, do it yourself.

ADD YOUR OWN!

Comfort

Good looking, single, soft-shelled turtle looking for never-married, 18-plus years, sensitive, attractive, intelligent, same shell structure.

I have excellent communication and listening skills, no vices, good health. I also have a secluded home with hot tub, hiking trails, and areas for meditation. Will consider sharing shell when mutually agreed upon, willing to commit to a prehabitation agreement.

Control

Looking for someone who is flexible, pleasing, tolerant, humble, nonjudgmental, a follower, a good listener, fun, challenging but persuadable, spontaneous, creative, exciting, and who can cook, clean, does windows, and follows directions well.

Pleasing

Looking for roommate(s). Any warm, live body. I'm flexible, willing to accommodate. Any circumstances. Prefer nonsmoker (I have fan), drinker or nondrinker. Children, animals OK. Willing to adapt to any lifestyle. No rent necessary; employment not required—willing to subsidize your income. Enjoy cultural differences. Either sex. Willing to resettle if you're not pleased. Contact me anytime 24-hours-a-day, every day. 1-800-LUV-ALL! References not necessary.

Superiority

Don't read anymore unless you meet the following requirements:

Genuine, Eclectic, Nonjudgmental (just helpful), Intelligent, Unbeatable, and Successful (in other words, a **GENIUS**)
I possess all the above traits as well as being the best lover you have ever experienced. If you are serious about getting involved in a meaningful, committed relationship, call 1-800-THE-BEST. Do not waste my time!

3. What if you were going to create a business that reflected your top card? What would it be called? Describe it. Create a slogan for it. Who would your prospective customers be? What would your phone number be? For inspiration, check out some of the ideas others have come up with.

Comfort top card business

Company Name: Turtle Spa

Description of Product or Service: Relaxation spa with massage, sauna, therapy, hot tubs, mud baths, and food.

Slogan: Slow down with us.

Prospective Customers: Anyone looking for simple solutions to difficult problems. People who have all the time and money they want without ever really trying. Anyone who was born rich, marries rich, has a rich attitude, and likes to plan the fun stuff first, delegate, get help, and have uninterrupted peace and quiet with time for personal moaning and groaning.

Phone Number: 1-LESS-STRESS or 1-900-TUR-TLES

Superiority top card business

Company Name: Coulda, Woulda, Shoulda Consultants, Inc.

Description of Product or Service: Computerized tracking of time and money. We'll make all the decisions for you and provide a 24-hour personal manager to accompany you everywhere. We'll make sure you don't make any mistakes, and we won't criticize you unless you really deserve it. We provide workshops, books, cassettes, videos, electronic mail, and other educational tools to help you learn what is best for you. All messages are crystal clear in black and white, right or wrong, and all or nothing.

Slogan: We know what's best for you. Let us put the brakes on your mistakes.

Prospective Customers: You'll find our services helpful if you would like to find time for yourself, get ideas on how to increase your wealth, learn to work smarter, not harder, and are willing to put us in the driver's seat. A percentage of every dollar you spend will be donated to a worthwhile cause to make our world better. Don't waste time. Make your activities meaningful and filled with purpose. Do the right thing and call us today.

Phone Number: 1-800-NO-WASTE or 1-800-THE-BEST.

Pleasing top card business

Company Name: Margaritaville Cruises.

Description of Product or Service: Cruises anywhere you like. Everything you want to make your life hassle-free. A great escape from reality.

Slogan: Don't worry, be happy. Your needs are our deeds. Yes!

Prospective Customers: Anyone who enjoys a group of warm and friendly people taking care of all of your needs. All opinions and philosophies welcome.

Phone Number: 1-800-WE-PLEAS or 1-800-YES-2-YOU.

Control top card business

Company Name: Eagle Enterprises

Description of Product or Service: Time management consultants, business organizers, and bodyguard services. Manufacturers of subliminal tapes, binoculars, and other tracking devices. Custom license plates such as BACKOFF, OUTAMWA, MKMYDAY, LVMALON.

Slogan: Soar to new heights. My way or the highway!

Prospective Customers: If you would like to gain control and respect and avoid criticism and humiliation from administrators and colleagues, we can help you. We will assist you in becoming more effective leaders and crisis managers, or if needed, we'll create a crisis for you to manage.

Phone Number: 1-800-DEFENSV or 1-800-IN-CHARG.

4. Think of a recent time when you felt stressed. Write down what you did to deal with the situation. Look at the top card behaviors on the chart on page 43 and see if you played your top card. Use the methods on pages 45-47 to help you track down your fear, find your underlying issues, and work with them. If you don't face your fears, you'll end up with what you are trying to avoid. Think about the boxes you used to find out what your top card was. Look in those boxes to remind yourself of what is in store for you if you use a defensive top card behavior instead of dealing with the situation by facing your fears.

5. Write out the answers to the following questions:

   ☑ How does your top card bring you success?

   ☑ How does your top card create problems for you?

   ☑ What do you want to or need to work on?

Review the sections on how people with your top card made changes and pick something you could work on this week.

 <u>Week 3</u>

Use Your Top Card to Improve Relationships

When you or others are discouraged and play your top cards, you can wreak havoc in relationships. You make situations worse instead of better when you are scared and respond to a perceived threat by operating in your survival mode. This week, you will learn what to do if your actions result in contentious relationships instead of peaceful ones. You will also discover how to deflect other people's discouragement so you can invite harmony into your relationships. As you read the following four stories, think about two things: First, do you ever act the way Millie, Clark, Charlene and Tony do, and second, how do you respond to someone behaving like them?

Millie, for no apparent reason, withdraws emotionally and becomes rejecting and vengeful. If anyone asks her what's wrong she says, "Nothing," with a tone that implies the opposite. Millie's top card is Pleasing, but when she plays it, she is anything but pleasing.

Clark, who is normally even-tempered, can without warning, act angry, controlling, and critical of everyone around him. Clark has a Control top card, and when he plays it, he is out of control.

Charlene keeps herself busy doing things that do not really need to be done, while thinking constantly about what a failure she is. If anyone asks what is going on, she puts herself or the other person down until they leave her alone. Charlene's top card is Superiority, but she really feels inadequate when she plays her top card.

Tony snaps at a simple request and then shuts down, refusing to talk about what is bothering him. He has been known to walk off in a huff, leaving everyone around with mouths agape. His top card is Comfort/Avoidance, although no one is very comfortable when he walks off in anger.

The people who live and work with Millie, Clark, Charlene, and Tony do not have a clue as to what is going on when faced with these behaviors, so they react in ways that make the situation worse. This week the focus of *Do-It-Yourself Therapy* takes **two** different paths. You can choose one or both to help you become encouraging and proactive rather than discouraging and reactive.

The first path offers seven suggestions to help you **get** the kind of nourishment you need when you are stressed so you can improve your situation. You'll invite others to treat you better when you become proactive, assertive, and balance your everyday style.

The second path demonstrates how to **give** the appropriate nurturing to people when they are at their worst so relationships move toward understanding. The second path contains information about how to meet the needs of others. When people feel cared for, they respond more cooperatively. The more you grasp this material and try the suggestions, the more effective you will be with family, friends, co-workers and loved ones.

Look at the chart on page 66 to see how you and others might act under stress as you play your top cards. Notice how different you are when you are at your worst and when you are at your best. The more stressed, threatened or scared you feel, the more likely you are to use

(!) Hint   The top card zoological reserve

If you are feeling hesitant working with the material in this chapter, try this: You have just been hired to work at a beautiful new zoo.

What might happen if you put turtles in the lions' cage, lions in an aviary, a chameleon in with the bobcats, or an eagle in a small, enclosed cage?

When it was feeding time, wouldn't you want to make sure that each animal was given the proper nourishment? When dealing with people who are playing their top cards, remember that their needs are as different as those of the animals in the zoo.

The more you are able and willing to give the care appropriate to their uniqueness, the better life works for everyone.

Top cards at your best and worst		
Top card	At your worst, you are:	At your best, you are:
Control	Trying to control everything. Defensive. Fault-finding. Cautious and withdrawn. Inviting power struggles. Catastrophizing and overdoing.	Coordinating activities. A great crisis manager. Patient and persevering. Loyal and helpful. Objective. Getting tasks done quickly.
Superiority	A know-it-all. Looking for blame. Not asking for help or input. Vertical view of relationships. Makes others feel useless.	Creative. Idealistic. A self starter. Independent and capable. Clear about what is important.
Comfort/ Avoidance	Hiding out. Biting others' heads off. Focused on comforts of others. Wasting your talents. Quiet.	Going with the flow. Able to express feelings. Supportive, helpful, and reliable. Persistent and fun-loving. Creative.
Pleasing	Too apologetic. Difficulty taking a stand. Losing your identity. Distrustful and easily hurt. Indirect.	Accepting and open minded. Adaptable. Genuinely interested in others. Good listener and optimistic. Empathetic.

your top card behaviors and be at your worst. The more inspired, coura-geous and bold you feel, the more you are apt to choose useful behaviors to be at your best. Think about the relationships where you are playing your top card at your worst. In which relationships are you playing your top card at your best? Consider how these behaviors might be impacting others and how people are relating to you as a result.

Kenny's story

Kenny has a Pleasing top card. It's always stressful for Kenny when he has to tell someone what he wants. He noticed that when his wife tells him what she wants, Kenny does anything to please her. He gives himself over completely, and agrees with her wishes instead of telling her that he has something else in mind. He believes if he is honest, she will make life difficult for him. But with his friend Max, Kenny does his pleasing. He has learned that Max is less apt to make hassles, so it's easier for Kenny to be accepting and open-minded with his own needs.

Feed upon emotional nourishment

Getting the emotional nourishment you need will reduce the amount of time you feel stressed. The suggestions in this section help you meet your needs so that you do not make your relationships worse. The first suggestion applies to your specific top card, while the rest will work for all of the top cards. Pick one of the suggestions and try it out for a short time (an hour, an evening, a day). Notice how you feel and what kind of responses you get from others. Then try out another suggestion, and then another. You will find what works best for you, allowing you to feel better, able to create the kind of relationships you want.

You may notice as you do your therapy this week that people around you respond in a variety of ways to your new behaviors. Some will be excited to see you feeling and working better, while others may feel threatened with your changes. Let people have their reactions without changing your course. Soon they will discover that your changes are not a danger to them. You may become an inspiration to some, especially if you do not try to change them or convince them that they should do what you are doing. The more energy you spend trying to make others change, the more energy they will spend trying to stay the same.

Suggestion 1: Be proactive instead of reactive

To get the nourishment you need, catch yourself playing your top card and, as quickly as possible, replace your reactive coping behaviors with one of the choices from the guidelines below. Last week you began learning how to catch yourself playing your top card. If you need extra help, use the "Top cards at your best and worst" chart on page 66 to help you. Any small step you take that creates patterns that are less reactive and more proactive will help you succeed with your therapy. These new patterns will reduce your stress, and invite others to treat you respectfully.

Guidelines for being proactive when under stress

CONTROL
- ☑ Remind yourself that you are not responsible for everyone.
- ☑ Stop trying to prevent problems you don't have.

☑ Stop and listen to others instead of withdrawing.

☑ Think about what you want and then ask for it.

☑ Listen instead of getting defensive.

☑ Ask for help and choices.

☑ Delegate.

SUPERIORITY

☑ Stop looking for blame and start working on solutions.

☑ Give credit where credit is due, including to yourself.

☑ Look at what you have instead of what you don't have.

☑ Show an interest in others and be curious about them.

☑ Create balance in your life by walking, exercising, or eating something healthy.

COMFORT

☑ Create a routine for yourself.

☑ Show up and stick around, even if all you do at first is watch.

☑ Speak up, ask questions, or say what you want.

☑ Tell others how you are feeling.

☑ Ask someone to do things with you at your pace till you feel comfortable.

PLEASING

☑ Be more honest and say what you are thinking and feeling.

☑ Say no and mean it.

☑ Let others have their feelings and let their behavior be about them and not you.

☑ Spend time alone and give up trying to please everyone.

☑ Don't be afraid to ask for help or for another perspective.

Suggestion 2: Know your everyday style

Becoming aware of your everyday style is yet another tool for noticing how you are around others, how they are affected by your behavior, and how you can invite more harmonious relationships. Remember that you play your top card when you feel afraid to avoid rejection and hassles, criticism and humiliation, pain and stress, or meaninglessness and unimportance. Your everyday style is the way you operate in life the rest of the time. Although you always have all four cards available for your daily use, your everyday style is most familiar. You continue using your everyday style until you are faced with one of your stressors, then you play your top card to stay safe.

Every person has access to all the top card behaviors in his or her everyday styles. However, one style is dominant. To find your dominant everyday style is, think about your second choice top card or look at the chart on page 70 to explore which behaviors you use most of the time.

If you have a Pleasing top card and a Control everyday style, you might use any of the behaviors in the Control column regularly. When stressed, you use your Pleasing top card behaviors to protect yourself. If your top card is Control and you have a Pleasing everyday style, you might use any of the behaviors in the Pleasing column frequently, and when you are afraid, you use Control top card behaviors. Any and all combinations are possible, and none are better or worse. Each combination affects the balance in your everyday life and your relationships.

Suggestion 3: Balance in your everyday style

Although you may have a dominant everyday style, you can also have elements of all four top cards in your daily style. You may have already realized that some of these behaviors are very handy to have at certain times. When you are able to create a balance of Comfort, Superiority, Control and Pleasing in your life, you will be surprised at how much better you feel.

Candace's story

Candace's life revolved around her family, friends, work, and extended family. She constantly tried to figure out what others wanted so that she would be loved and accepted. However, her behavior resulted in depression, migraines, bouts with overeating and overdrinking, and feelings of isolation and loneliness.

(!) **Hint**   Your everyday style: Why you do what you do

You will abandon your everyday style in favor of your top card when scared, stressed or threatened. As you read the chart, try filling in the following:

"My top card is _____ and my everyday style is _____.

When I operate with my everyday style, I use these behaviors: (choose those that fit from the chart)."

Everyday Styles			
Control	Superiority	Pleasing	Comfort
Hold things inside, stay very quiet, try to cover all your bases, organize others, give instructions and information, be a crisis manager, fix things for others, take control of all situations, take over, manage everyone and everything, overdo, catastrophize.	Blame yourself, feel responsible for everything, try to obtain the best of everything, intellectualize, attack when challenged, catastrophize, get annoyed when others don't listen to your good ideas, try harder and harder and do more and more, go along until it is no longer meaningful to you and then do it your way.	Let others decide what to do, socialize, laugh, joke, cheer others on, don't say what you really want, think or feel, take care of everyone, go last, sacrifice for others and then quietly resent them later, try to make everyone happy.	Keep a low profile, be easy-going, act diplomatic and predictable, avoid situations where someone might be unhappy or upset, hide out, take the path of least resistance, make things harder than they look, figure out ways to avoid doing what you don't want to do, wait until you are ready, block your feelings, and go at your own pace.

As she worked on her therapy, one day she discovered something very important: inside of her was a person who knew what she wanted. This was a bit of a shock to her, as she realized she almost always knew what everyone else wanted but was unaware of her own needs. She realized that she would never ignore anyone else the way she had been ignoring her own needs.

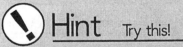 Hint   Try this!

Draw a circle and divide it into four sections that reflect how much of each of the everyday styles are currently reflected in your life.

Use the "Everyday Styles" chart above to review the different everyday styles. If your circle is heavy in one area and light in another, you might want to think about adding more of the behaviors of that style to your life.

Initially, when she drew her circle, seven/
eighths of it was Pleasing, there was no Comfort,
no Superiority, and only one/eighth of Control.
Candace realized how out-of-balance she was.

Several months after she began to work on
her relationship with herself, by honoring the
person inside who knew what she wanted, she
redrew her circle. To her amazement it was now
divided into equal thirds with Pleasing, Control,
and Superiority filling each of the sections.

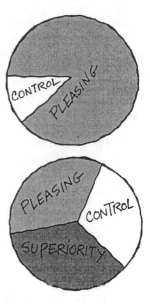

She was worrying less about what others
wanted (a reduction in Pleasing), saw that she
had more choices (an increase of Control), and
had more meaning and spirituality to her life (an
increase in Superiority). Even though this was a
definite improvement, her circle was still out of
balance. Candace resolved to figure out ways to
increase the Comfort segment. She began by asking for more help at work
and at home. When she felt both were running smoothly, took her first
solo vacation to a health spa, where she was pampered from head to toe.

Suggestion 4: Know what you want

Here's a simple way to practice being assertive: If something is on
your mind, say it out loud to the person who needs to hear it. Being assertive is not intended to change others (even though change is a result of this
practice). Being assertive is different from being aggressive, where the purpose of your behavior may be to win or to prove you are right. People with
different top cards view the world from different perspectives, so being assertive is a perfect way to make your perspective known instead of relating
to others through assumptions. People are not mind readers.

April's story

"I was having a difficult time getting along with a neighbor of mine. I
realized that I was being very quiet about what bothered me. I was afraid to
talk to her about it because I didn't want to make waves. Finally, I decided
that I would just bring it up. What helped me was to understand that I was
afraid because I don't like problems, and that my behavior was pretty normal for someone with a Comfort top card. Once I knew what my issue was,
I did a quick reality check and remembered that this neighbor is usually

quite open about working on solutions. That made it easier for me to take a risk and tell her what was bothering me. When I did, she laughed, because to her it was such a little thing that could be easily remedied. For me, speaking up replaced my discomfort with positive action."

Suggestion 5: Review your priorities

This exercise in prioritizing helps you avoid stressful situations by realizing what is important to you. By the time you reach adulthood, you learned to not listen to your inner voice that knows what you want. The result is a state of stress as you try to live according to someone else's whims.

We find many of the activities available for establishing goals and action plans to be too tedious and complex. Our method focuses on discovering what your priorities are. With such awareness, whatever needs to happen will happen, without you having to work at it.

To discover your priorities, take out a piece of paper and write down the following four headings spaced down the left hand side of the page:

1. How I would like my life to be five years from now?
2. What do I would do if I had just one month to live?
3. How do I typically spend my time?
4. My thoughts about what I just wrote.

To adjust your perspective, go back to question number one and picture how old you and the important people around you will be five years from now. This helps you be more realistic about how long five years is. Then write down three to five statements about how you would like your life to be. Don't think too much. Now, answer questions two and three in the same way. Look over your answers to questions one through three and write two to three comments after question number four.

The next part of the activity may seem strange, but it will make sense once you do it. Completely black out questions one and two (just the

(!) Hint   Don't expect others to read your mind

Some people think that if they have to ask for what they want, getting it will not mean anything. If you do not ask for what you want, no one can read your mind, and you may be sitting around forever, wishing others would know what you are thinking.

questions, not the answers you wrote) and then, starting at the top of the page and finishing at the bottom, number your answers starting with number one, making a single numbered list. Title your list "My Priorities." Look at the paper, reread what you wrote. Then throw it out, place it in a drawer, or tuck it between the pages of a book. That's all you need to do to realign yourself. Someday, you may stumble onto this paper, and you will probably be quite surprised to see that many, if not most of your wishes have become realities in your life. You can use Lilah's priorities on page 74 as a guide.

Lilah's story

"When I did this activity, I noticed I was happy with what I was doing but not the way I was conducting my life. Everything felt rushed and crammed in and I was spending too much time trying to be nice instead of doing what I wanted. I realize that this is not unusual for someone with my Pleasing top card. I decided to tell everyone around me I needed time alone and wanted their help with this so that I could give up being 'hostess' or 'program director.' I changed my schedule around, and I was amazed at how everyone wanted to help me make my new schedule work. I guess they were more aware than I was of just how stressed I had been lately.

Knowing that my real priority is to have a more relaxed and enjoyable pace with more flexibility has been a great help to me. As for the stress about money, I'm hoping that being more aware will work to take away some of my panic, without having to come up with a new budget and savings plan."

Suggestion 6: Take time for training

When you want to make a change, you often spend a lot of time at the beginning of the process—figuring out what problem you want to work on, and then coming up with a plan for making your situation

(!) Hint Feelings aren't good or bad

There are no positive or negative feelings. It is acceptable to feel any way you do. Stop judging your feelings and remember that feelings are different from actions and that how you feel does not cause how you act.

Example: Lilah's Priorities

1. ~~How I would like my life to be five years from now~~:
   1. Choose what I do without worrying about money.
   2. Spend fun time with my kids frequently.
   3. Be physically involved in the sport of the day.
   4. Good health for me and my loved ones.
2. ~~What I would do if I had just one month to live~~:
   5. ~~1.~~Treat everyone I love to a week in Hawaii.
   6. ~~2.~~Put my affairs in order.

— —

3. How I typically spend my time:
   1. Working, working, working, cramming in new activities, and feeling stressed.
   2. Hanging out with friends and family when they want to and when I can.
   3. Trying to respond to everybody's needs.
   4. Cramming in exercise when there is time.
   5. Commuting twelve hours a week.
4. My thoughts about what I just wrote:
   1. I do what I like but I try to cram everything in instead of enjoying it and I'm stressed.
   2. I worry too much about money, work too hard and have less time for the activities that are important to me.
   3. I'm doing a lot but I don't have a lot of flexibility.
   4. It's not what I do but how I do it that is the problem.

---

better. Like most people, you may forget the back end of the process, which we call "time for training." Let's look at a simple way to make "time for training" part of your therapy this week.

Start by identifying the problem you want to work on. Without doing anything different, spend a day or two observing how events are currently proceeding. Pay attention to what happens if you do absolutely nothing about the problem for a few days. Some of you may discover that you have been spending a lot of time and effort trying to change others and failing miserably. Just stopping behaviors that have not been working may already have changed the situation for the better.

Next, tell someone else what you have noticed or write yourself a note or journal entry and reread it for more clarity. Now, think of something you could do that would make your situation better or ask someone else for a suggestion. Decide what you will do differently and plan to do it for a week. Even though you have done a lot of work, you are still at the front-end of the process.

The back-end of making changes, "time for training," is the time it takes to learn the new skill or pattern. It's the time you spend putting your plan into action, taking your steps to see how they feel by practicing, feeling awkward, feeling relieved, then giving yourself permission to be less than perfect. No one makes a decision to do something differently and has everything fall into place immediately. Without time for training, the changes you start by planning will soon disintegrate.

Harley's story

Harley started working for a company that wanted all the employees to use the computer network for tracking new business. He was good at his job and had always found ways to get things done without using a computer. He resisted working with the system and instead tried to convince others that everything could be done in writing or by communicating orally. This worked until orders for his company's products started flooding in. He was not sleeping nights, worrying about keeping up with delivering products as promised. He realized that unless he used the computer system, all his efforts at sales would be subverted when customers became angry that their orders were not filled. For someone who liked to be in control, this was truly a nightmare.

Harley went to his supervisor and told him about his anxiety. The supervisor smiled and said, "Harley, that's what your computer is for. We're all on a network, and when you enter something into the product management program, it pops up on all your backup people's screens. We're here to help you, but we can't respond to your needs unless they pop up on our screens when we log on to our computers. Do you need help learning how to use the system?"

Harley knew he did not need help; what he needed was intention and time. Now that he was committed to the new program, he set up time to learn the new system. Every day after his colleagues went home, Harley sat at the computer for several hours, struggling to enter the data and learn the system. He even went to the office on weekends to bring himself up to speed. Up until now, he had been sharp enough to fake his way through a lot of different jobs, but this time, he wanted to put in the time to learn the skill that would help him be part of the bigger system and eventually, he did.

Suggestion 7: Make a strong recovery

No one makes changes in relationships without taking some steps backwards, and it's entirely normal to be in recovery and relapse at the same time. Recovery is the process of becoming healthier, more aware, and proactive. If you hardly have the energy to focus on anything, or if you are not taking good care of yourself, you may be in a state which we call relapse. To "fill up your cup" and recover, you need to do more to demonstrate love for your own self. This love is different for each person, so give some thought to what nourishes you and what depletes you. If you are not sure what makes you feel better, start paying attention to how you feel after you do something. Ask yourself, "Does this activity give me energy, or does it drain me?" In this way, you can begin to discover ways to show love for yourself.

Alissa's story

Alissa's attempts at do-it-yourself therapy were like riding a roller coaster: Some days she was on top of the world. Others, she was at the bottom with an upset stomach, trying to regain her equilibrium. On her good days she got work done, attended a t'ai chi class, and made time to visit a friend. On her bad days, she stayed in bed with the shades drawn, thinking about how depressing and meaningless her life was.

The idea of being in recovery and relapse at the same time seemed completely ridiculous to Alissa, who was a black and white, either/or thinker with a Superiority top card. But she decided to keep a chart of the activities that gave her energy (the plus side) and the ones that brought her down (the minus side). After a week, it was apparent to Alissa that most of her activities were "downers." She decided to do the obvious and add more activities that energized her. She reorganized her files, made up a budget for her new business, looked for office space, quit a part-time job she hated, called five client leads a day and added jogging to her exercise program. She still spent too much time at home alone and continued to tell herself that she would never get her new business started. However, as her recovery (the positive) side of the list began to outweigh the relapse (the negative) side, she noticed that she was feeling better.

Keep a stone in your pocket

Another very helpful and very simple way to work on top card is to carry a top card stone in your pocket or give one to a friend. The stones have the picture of your top card animal on one side and the

"I CAN DO WHAT I WANT"   "I'M SPECIAL"   "I'M GREAT"   "I CAN"

words of encouragement you need on the other. They are colorful, light-weight and magical. Look above to see four examples. When you feel bad, take out your stone, hold it in your hand, read the words to yourself, put it back and notice how much better you feel. The Control stone says "I can do what I want." You will find "I'm special" on the Superiority stone. The Pleasing stone asserts, "I'm great," while the Comfort stone reminds, "I can."

Working with each top card dealt

In this part of the chapter, you follow the second path and learn to be encouraging and proactive, instead of discouraging and reactive. This path shows you how to focus on others in order to move relationships towards understanding instead of conflict. You will learn how to nurture people with each of the four top cards when they are at their worst. Their needs are very distinct, so tailoring your approach to the uniqueness of each top card can make a huge difference with a minimum effort on your part.

Because each top card has a different style, a separate reality, and a distinctive perspective, it's amazing that two people ever see anything the same way or get along at all. Notice how various top cards interact in the following stories.

Merle and Stan's story

Merle's top card is Pleasing and Stan's is Comfort. On the surface this combination might seem ideal. However, Merle never says how she really feels about anything, and is busy trying to please her partner. Stan avoids dealing with issues. Merle and Stan have fallen into a habit of doing what is familiar and comfortable. A discussion about going out to dinner might sound like this:

"Where do you want to go to dinner, honey?" Stan asks. "Oh, anywhere you want, I don't care." "Well, you know I like Buffy's Beef House," he says. "That's fine with me, whatever you want," answers Merle, in spite of the fact that she prefers eating low-fat foods. Merle does not tell the truth for fear of upsetting Stan and causing a hassle, so Stan does not have a clue that there is a problem.

Many months later, the usual discussion about going out to dinner leads to an outburst from Merle that shocks them both. "I hate Buffy's Beef House," Merle screamed. "It's filled with food drenched in fat!" With that she burst into tears and ran into the bedroom. Stan stood in the kitchen, hurt and shocked. Not knowing where her outburst came from or what to do, he went into the family room and turns on the TV.

Luis and Marty's story

Control/Control is a frequent and interesting combination, and as you might guess, one that can lead to conflict. When both people have a Control top card and want to be in control of every situation without criticism and ridicule, the result can be angry power struggles. Luis and Marty work together. Luis is the manager and Marty works in the sales department.

Marty thought of himself as the "Boy Scout Salesman" because his motto was "Be Prepared," and he resented all the busy work his boss Luis gave him. Instead of talking to Luis about his anger, he kept things to himself, appearing to be responding to Luis' demands while actually putting him off. This is passive power, the art of looking good while doing bad, or telling people what they want to hear while doing exactly the opposite.

When Luis tried to prove he was the boss by burying Marty in paperwork, Marty's favorite expression was, "Luis, I'll be bringing in that project you wanted in a few days." Marty always had a smile on his face, but he was burning up inside. He did not mind putting in extra time to prepare for an appointment with a buyer. But he was not willing to satisfy Luis' need for power by doing extra work.

It's not too surprising that Marty eventually developed an ulcer. Passive resistance drains energy and ignored feelings frequently manifest themselves somewhere else in the body. For all his autocratic efforts to control Marty, Luis still did not get what he wanted. This is a typical pattern when Control meets Control—both pay attention to who will win, rather than looking for solutions together.

Darlene and Roy's story

Darlene, whose top card was Control, lived with her boyfriend, Roy, whose top card was Superiority. In the beginning of their six years together, they felt comfortable because Roy liked people who stood up for themselves so he couldn't become a tyrant. Darlene liked people who put everything "out there," which made it easier for her to know what she had to deal with. Over the years, they started experiencing some problems when the same behaviors that attracted them to each other started to distress them.

Roy was always "right" about everything and Darlene was constantly trying to take charge. They bumped heads on many issues. Darlene felt put down, criticized and inadequate a good part of the time. Roy was feeling constantly challenged, frustrated, and unappreciated—certainly not the feelings that lead to a long-lasting, healthy relationship. Darlene and Roy knew something was wrong but did not know what. They loved each other and decided to get some help to see if they could make their relationship work.

Joan and Mary Lou's story

In another common top card combination, Joan, who had a Superiority top card, and her friend Mary Lou, who had a Comfort top card, learned how their two styles meshed. They met once a week to visit while their five-year-old girls played together. Joan's daughter, Abigail, always looked perfect. Every hair was in place and her outfits always matched, down to her ruffled socks and patent leather "Mary Janes." Looking like a little princess, she sat quietly and played with one toy at a time.

Mary Lou's daughter Vicky wore jeans, a sweatshirt, and tennis shoes. She would pull out one toy after another and run circles around Abigail. Joan watched this and thought to herself, "How can she let her daughter behave like that? She's wild." Mary Lou seemed to take no notice of her daughter's behavior as she continued her conversation with Abigail.

> **(!) Hint**   Disagreeing is healthy when it is respectful
>
> In relationships, it is normal for people to think differently from each other. But when there is no room in the relationship to disagree, neither person reveals his or her true feelings, making it impossible to resolve issues or develop intimacy or real closeness. The suppressed feelings develop into resentments that grow over time and surface either indirectly or directly, usually in a disrespectful way.

When Joan and Mary Lou decided to take a parenting class based on Positive Discipline ideas to learn about children's behavior and how to be effective and respectful parents, they also learned about top card. (Rudolf Dreikurs and Vicki Soltz in their book, *Children: The Challenge*, introduced these Positive Discipline ideas, which are based on mutual respect.) They began to see how their reactions were inviting some of the difficulties they were having. Joan recognized how she was discouraging Abigail because she had such high expectations for her to look and be perfect. Abigail was afraid to make a move for fear of getting messy, spilling or making a mistake. Joan's efforts to motivate success were backfiring and she did not understand why. On the other hand, Mary Lou saw how her laissez-faire attitude was creating a tyrant who was increasingly demanding, out-of-control, and unpleasant to be around.

As the two women discussed what they were learning, they were surprised to find that they admired some of the characteristics of the other's behavior. Joan shared how much she wished she could be as easy-going and relaxed as Mary Lou, and Mary Lou shared that she admired how self-confident Joan seemed. They realized what a good combination Superiority and Comfort could be and how they could help each other.

First things first

One of the simplest ways to make positive headway with a person playing a top card is to say, "I notice you are (*describe the behavior*). That's probably how you behave when you're feeling scared, threatened, or stressed. Can you tell me what's bothering you right now?" For example, with the Control top card you might say, "I notice you're being critical..." For the Superiority top card you might say, "I notice you're putting me/yourself down and/or making me/yourself/the situation meaningless..." For the Pleasing top card you might say, "I notice you're being rejecting..." For the Comfort top card you might say, "I notice you're causing a lot of stress and pain right now..."

Instead of fighting or fleeing, choose a different, more cooperative behavior. The more proactive you are, the more you allay potentially difficult situations. You will be able to help your eagle turn into a friendly parakeet, your lion into a kitten, a chameleon into a cuddle toy, and a snapping turtle into a house pet.

For specific "care and feeding" plans for each top card, read on. These plans were designed at a workshop where participants were divided into groups by top card. They were asked a series of questions about what they needed to help them when they are in their top card behaviors.

Nurturing people with Control top cards

The suggestions the group with Control top cards made are in list form. There is no order of importance. Making lists for people with Control top cards can be helpful, but ask them first if they want you to do this. People with Control top cards like it when you give them choices or tell them what the rules are. However, do not change the rules midway. People with Control top cards do not like change!

1. "I need you to be a friend in order to feel connected to you. However, once I have a close relationship with you, when I'm in a mess, anything you do that looks like you are pointing a finger at me will feel like criticism. What helps me is for you to be there physically without trying to fix anything, or for you to use nonverbal signals, such as a gentle touch on my shoulder, a hug, a hand on my knee, or a smile. Just be present or touch me to help me get back into my body. These are ways I know you love and support me, and then I feel free to fix what I need to."

2. "If you ask me, 'How's it going?' or 'How do you feel?' it's tough for me to answer because I probably don't know. I can make up an answer so you'll be happy, but it's pretty meaningless. I need help to be sensitive. Allow me to have the time I need to figure out that I'm having a feeling, that it has a name, and then I can tell you. It might take me a day, a week, or a month, so please don't rush me."

3. "I prepare and prepare because if something isn't organized, I'm behind and overwhelmed. I like to catch my mistakes by myself. Don't ask me to explain myself or I'll just get defensive. It's best to come to me in a gentle nonconfrontational way to find out what is going on with me."

4. "If you observe something, acknowledge it without judgment and accept me as I am. It makes it easier to accept myself."

5. "You can help me get what I want by backing off. Don't say you want me to do what I want, and then act like you don't really mean it by hovering nearby or asking me to do things for you. I want to be helpful, and I don't want to be criticized. So, if you make a request, I'm more likely to do what you ask than take care of myself."

6. "I can be high maintenance because sometimes I'm really slow, but I can learn new skills. Help me by creating routines for me and holding me accountable. The repetition helps ground me."

7. "Give me permission to do what I want. Tell me what you are going to do or what the rules are; don't tell me what to do."

Nurturing people with Superiority top cards

These suggestions are in an either/or form, which is how most people with Superiority top cards view the world. People with this top card want the following from you when they are being difficult, intense, or irrational.

Do's

1. "Realize you are wrong and admit it."
2. "Say, 'Maybe I forgot something really important to you or that you wanted done a certain way. Is there a time we can sit down so I can give you my full attention and we can figure out some solution that is respectful to both of us?'"
3. "Say, 'You have your style and you are entitled to it. I don't want to have your style. I won't push my style on you. Please don't push your style on me.' "
4. "Say, 'You are right, and I'm not going to do it that way.' We love to hear we are right."
5. "Say, 'I must not understand what you understand, so could you tell me again.' "
6. "Show your real feelings to me instead of hiding them or talking about them."
7. "When we are discouraged, remind us about what we have already accomplished."
8. "Remind us that everyone makes mistakes and that a mistake is not the end of the world."
9. "Use your sense of humor and lighten up the situation."
10. "Compliment us and show us appreciation. We love that if it is sincere."

Don'ts

1. "If you have attacked us, we don't want to hear your feelings at that time. Just listen and apologize for hurting us, even if it was inadvertent."
2. "Don't bother with indirect fighting because we will see right through you."
3. "Don't try to help or fix us because we can fix ourselves. Simply give information and let us do the rest."

4. "Don't ask, 'How are you feeling?' because we don't think feelings are important, or may expect you to know this information already."

5. "If we say 'No, that's it,' don't keep asking in different ways to get us to change our minds. If you cross our lines, we will write you off or fight you. If we think we have clearly communicated with you already, we won't talk to you, because that's a waste of time. We want our space." (If you are in this situation, try Number 2 or Number 5 from the "Do's" List.)

6. "Do not get too serious with us when we are serious, unless you want the situation to go downhill."

7. "Don't expect us to show an interest in you or your perspective. But, if we are being rude or self-centered, do tell us that and give us an example of what you want instead."

Nurturing people with Pleasing top cards

You'll notice that this is the shortest section. People with Pleasing top cards never seem to know what they really want until they are right in the middle of a situation and then it's too late.

"Know us more than we know ourselves. Don't take advantage of us. Keep your promises or don't make them in the first place unless you can be counted on to do as you say. Let us know we can have what we want without hurting you. Apologize for not appreciating us. Appreciate us, but make sure you are specific about what you appreciate. Remember that we hate feeling rejected, so treat us as if we matter. Ask questions about us and don't talk about yourself all the time. We know when we are being brats, but we hope you will think of us as cute and adorable and tease us instead of attacking us.

"When we ask for help, take us seriously and give us help with the things that seem like hassles to us. Don't help us if we don't ask for help, because then we have to figure out how to tell you you're in our space without hurting your feelings. Take responsibility for your own behavior. If you want something, tell us clearly and directly, as we love to please but hate to guess at unexpressed feelings. Create a life for yourself so that you are not always in our space. We need time alone, because often it is the only time we think it is okay to do what we want without hurting someone's feelings, or getting into some kind of trouble."

Nurturing people with Comfort top cards

People with Comfort top cards often wait to feel better. They do not believe they can make positive changes. This is far from the truth, as people with Comfort cards are quite resourceful. Waiting does not change anything. If those with Comfort top cards want change they have to do the work. What they really need is help to do the work as soon as possible. Your job will be figuring out the ways you can help. Be careful not to do the work for them; you could end up co-dependent, hopeless, or angry with their pace. The following do's and don'ts can serve as a guide for how to be helpful without taking over.

Do's

1. "If you want me to do something, give me a lot of information ahead of time. If you ask me to go on a hike, I need to know what the temperature will be, how long the hike is, what kind of clothing to wear, whether I need to carry food, water, and so forth. Then, I can know ahead of time that if I get into an uncomfortable place or situation, I'll have what I need to get out of it."

2. "Talk with me about what we're doing before we start, making sure there are choices, and that I get to participate in the decision-making process. Unless I believe an activity is safe, I won't do it. I want to be able to say 'I will' or 'I won't' without anyone being mad at me. I always need to know I have an escape route."

3. "I need to be appreciated for my own thoughts and feelings. I want to be taken seriously and not discounted."

4. "I need to slow down when I'm trying out new behaviors. An extra minute or two (or sometimes years) gives me time to process all of the information."

5. "When I feel stressed, I want two things that seem opposite: I want help and I want to be left alone. I can get both if someone knows how to be a support system at those moments when I am really stressed. They need to be encouraging and comforting for just a few minutes to help me over the hump. I like it when they say, 'I have faith in you,' or 'Take as long as you need—there's no rush.' "

6. "I would do best if I had a partner who would really listen, and be supportive, encouraging, and as fun and helpful as I am. We'd come together, get energy from each other, then go off and do our thing. I have to trust someone and feel safe."

7. "Sometimes all I need is a little boost, such as someone saying, 'Go ahead. What's the worst thing that could happen?' "

8. "Sometimes, I get in a spot where I keep my mouth shut because I think if I say anything, someone will say it's stupid, I'm stupid, or why don't I go off and do it myself. I'm always sizing up a situation and assessing the odds of getting to do what I want to do—try to make myself somewhat comfortable."

Don'ts

1. "It doesn't work to catch me by surprise or to pressure me into something. If all of a sudden I have to be a part of what someone else is doing or whatever else is happening, I won't want to."

2. "Don't try to get me out of denial. Sometimes I want to pretend everything is okay—I don't want to be coaxed."

3. "The worst thing someone can do is take charge, because then I feel as if I'm discounted and not appreciated."

Creating changes in your world

Top card information can he helpful, fun, and enlightening as long as it is never used as an accusation, a label, or in any other disrespectful way. This week create some time to try out some of the activities to help you increase your understanding and appreciation of the differences between the four top cards and everyday styles.

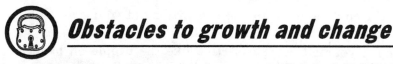

Obstacles to growth and change

1. If you forget that top cards are not good or bad, but that avoidance/protection behaviors are based on fear, you might attack, instead of stopping, thinking, and responding proactively.

2. If you forget that top card behaviors are what people do when stressed and not a statement of who they are, you could create a lot of distance between you and others.

3. You may forget that what people say is about them, and not about you.

4. When you make assumptions instead of checking out information, you end up with problems instead of solutions.

5. You could create many problems by thinking that everyone responds in the same way to different kinds of nurturing.

Easy steps for change

☑ Write a letter or use e-mail to communicate with someone you are having difficulties with. This form of dialogue gives you a perfect opportunity to be more proactive, think about what you want to say, make modifications before sending off your message, and cool off before replying to something sent your way.

☑ Take time to notice other people playing their top cards. Use the "Guidelines for being proactive when under stress" list on page 67 for help with this.

☑ If you notice you clash with certain individuals, you may find you are reacting to their top card behaviors. Maybe they are doing something you dislike about yourself. Perhaps as they play their top cards you feel competitive. Be an observer until you figure out what is going on.

☑ If people are willing, find out what their top cards are and then ask them to tell you what they need when stressed. You could show them the suggestions on pages 81-85 to help them with ideas.

☑ Compare your behaviors to the ones on the chart that shows top cards at their best and at their worst on page 66.

☑ Determine your primary or dominant everyday style, using the method shown on pages 68-71.

☑ Draw a circle and fill in the proportions of your everyday style as described on page 71.

☑ Imagine yourself being assertive like the people on pages 71-72. How would that change things for you?

☑ Work on revealing your priorities to yourself following the directions on pages 72-73.

Activities

1. Our much-quoted friend Steve Cunningham says, "We are attracted to other animals to build a peaceable kingdom, but when we try to change them, it's a jungle." Top cards remind us of the differences and uniqueness we all possess and that no one is better or worse—we are all just one of the kingdom. If you are feeling stuck, ask someone with a different

top card how he or she would handle the situation or deal with your particular problem.

2. As you meet people, remember that each person has a unique style. Guess which top card belongs with each person:

   A man sat on the sidewalk propped against a building reading a book while his dog lay in front of him with a sign around his neck pointing to a can in front of him that said, "Change?" (Comfort/Avoidance)

   Another man smiled as people walked by, saying, "Give as much as you can without leaving yourself short. God bless and have a good day!" (Pleasing)

   Another person stood in a doorway asking, "Can you spare some change." When people walked by and ignored him, he turned on them, started yelling and swearing at them. (Superiority)

   A woman sat on a blanket at the same spot every day, surrounded by her "stuff," and yelled at another panhandler who tried to intrude on her turf. (Control)

3. Think about someone with whom you have an important relationship. How do your top cards interact? Practice the art of understanding your different perspectives with mutual respect. Talk about what is important to each of you and try to consider each other's needs.

4. How are your automatic reactions working in your relationships? Are you getting what you want? Are you considering the needs of others? Try out some of the suggestions offered by each of the different top card groups to help nurture your relationships.

5. Make a list of as many items as you can think of that you are doing to enhance your recovery. List what you are doing that keeps you in relapse. Notice which list is longer and think of what you might change so that the recovery side grows.

6. Think about a recent time when you had a relationship difficulty with someone. Now think about your top card animal and, if you know it, the other person's top card animal. Replay the problem in your mind, picturing the animals interacting instead of the people. Write down your picture and what you learned from this experience.

 **Week 4**

Recognize How You Got to Be You

L ife is like a play. Each of you is an actor who was pushed out onto the stage in the middle of an act, required to improvise as you went along. (We were shown this often-used metaphor at a workshop presented by Amy Lew and Betty Lou Bettner.) From your first entrance, you ad-libbed from what you sensed inside you, what you saw around you, and what resulted from your interactions with your fellow players. Unaware that you were making decisions, you decided who and how you would have to be to remain distinct from the other characters, and you concluded how you would have to proceed to retain a role in the drama.

There is a long-standing debate on whether it is your genetic heritage or your childhood environment that has the most influence on your personality. In psychology, this pull between genes and society is called "nature versus nurture." Is it the inherited genetic makeup, or is it the situations, circumstances, and people to whom you relate that makes you who you are? While both are important, we use an additional parameter and consider it the most important factor. We believe it is the individual's unconscious decisions about what they bring with them and what happens around them that uniquely shapes their personalities.

Our formula for personalities

In your life, both your heredity and your environment influenced your unconscious decisions, but they did not create them. In order to give you a better idea of how your personality was developed, take a look at our formula below:

heredity + environment + unconscious decisions = personality
(nature)   (nurture)   (creative interpretations)

Heredity includes your genetics. Environment includes features that were present when you arrived: your parents, their values, their parenting style, their relationship with each other, your physical and social environment, your siblings, and your position in the birth order.

This week your therapy will take you back to your dramatic beginnings and expand your awareness of how your childhood relationships and experiences helped you shape your personality. As you understand more about how childhood events influenced your creative interpretations, you'll uncover some of your unconscious conclusions. Then, you can see how your childhood beliefs have taken you to success, and how they may also be creating problems for you. You may identify beliefs you want to modify.

The influence of your parents

As a child you stepped onto the stage of life, making your own decisions about yourself, others, life, and how to behave in order to belong. Your parents created the context for those decisions. (When we use the word "parents," we are referring to the adults who provided your primary care, whether they were your biological parents, stepparents, grandparents, baby sitters, and so forth.) They were the directors of the production, providing the environmental (nurture) part of the equation. They established the setting and atmosphere in the family. They communicated their values, from which you decided how people should and should not behave. The way they parented and disciplined you impacts all of your developing beliefs about yourself, others, life, and your own behavior. They provided siblings for you through birth, adoption, or marriage. We examine these environmental influences one by one to help you understand more about yourself.

Your environment's role in your personality

When you entered the play of your life, what was the set like? Was it filled with lots of people and noise? Did you grow up in a quiet, rural area? What language was spoken in your family or your neighborhood? What customs were observed? Were there lakes, rivers, mountains, plains, ocean dunes, or concrete? Your physical setting invites different kinds of decisions. If you grew up in an apartment in Manhattan, you'd probably have a different world view than someone who grew up in the Florida Everglades or on the plains of North Dakota.

Shirley's story

Shirley grew up in a Lutheran community in a small Midwestern town perched on the shore of one of the Great Lakes. Her family was the only Jewish family in the neighborhood, and she was frequently teased by the children in town. Shirley didn't know why the children did this to her—she thought they were her friends. How different Shirley's world view is from a Jewish child growing up in a predominantly Jewish neighborhood in a large metropolitan city. Shirley's beliefs about not fitting in were in part influenced by her childhood's setting.

The influence of a family's atmosphere

The stage was set before you were born. If someone described the atmosphere of your childhood, what would it be? Cheerful and happy? Gloomy and stormy? Orderly and predictable or chaotic and unpredictable? Scary or safe? Warm and friendly or cold and uninviting? This all had a profound effect on your feelings, expectations, and beliefs. Your family atmosphere was created by your parents, by the ways they related to each other, the ways they parented you, what they were like as people, and how they organized the household and the family.

Kevin and Joyce's story

Dishes crashed against the wall and silverware flew across the kitchen. This was a nightly occurrence at Kevin's house. He and his sister Joyce would take cover wherever they could. As their parents' drinking continued, screaming matches ensued. Evenings frequently ended with Kevin's father hitting his mother, who would fall asleep sobbing on the couch. The next morning they acted as if nothing had happened.

One day, Joyce went into Kevin's room to borrow scissors and glue. When Kevin verbally attacked her, Joyce called him names. Their bickering quickly escalated into a physical confrontation. Their mother was horrified when Joyce came to her screaming and bleeding because Kevin had thrown a toy truck at her, hitting her in the head. Kevin and Joyce's world was so chaotic and stormy as children, that it wasn't surprising that, as an adult, Kevin found himself sitting in a men's violence prevention group, while Joyce spent years as a battered wife.

The influence of your parents' values

Was the play of your life a comedy or tragedy? What was the story line or the major theme of your family's play? In all families, there are issues and topics of importance to both parents (when there are two), which we refer to as "family values." If you were raised by a single parent, perhaps many of your values came from grandparents or an extended community who helped to raise you. Whether the significant adults in your life were in agreement or not, you and your siblings got their messages one way or another.

Every family has values, but not all families' values are the same. Maybe you relate to some of these statements: "Work comes before play." "It's important to be physically fit." "Give to those less fortunate." "Don't say, don't tell, don't share." What are some of your family values? What were your family's values about illness, money, achievement, work, alcohol and drugs, sexuality, and male and female roles?

Your parents' attitudes about these and other issues were the themes of the thousands of interactions in your family when you were a child. You were exposed to those themes every day. Eventually, you either embraced the messages or rejected them. You rarely take a neutral stance with family values, so your decisions become the "shoulds" in the unconscious belief system that guides your life: "People *should* get a good education." "People *should* make sure they can be self-supporting." "People *should* be physically fit." "People *should* see to others before they take care of their own needs." "People *should* not be materialistic." "People *should* never discuss family business with strangers."

Denise and Mark's story

Denise grew up in a family where both parents thought a good education was essential to being a worthwhile human being. While neither of them put it in those words, they were both fascinated with their children's projects in school, attended every school function, and were upset when their children didn't work hard enough for good grades.

From the beginning, Denise's brother Mark did not do well at school. Every night Mark and his father battled over his homework. His father wanted it to be perfect before Mark turned it in. Mark, on the other hand, didn't seem to care about his homework and didn't understand what he was supposed to do. Although he managed to graduate from high school, Mark vowed to never set foot in a classroom again.

As a young man working in construction, Mark became a gifted craftsman with an eye for detail and was never satisfied until a project was completed perfectly. At the same time, he would not consider getting his own contractor's license because of the course work he'd have to take to sit for the licensing exam.

Denise, on the other hand, loved school. She took pride in her grades and the quality of her work. She chose college prep courses in high school, and attained an advanced university degree. Later in life, she took classes in what interested her as a way to expand her knowledge.

The influence of your parents' personalities

What were the lead adult players, or "parents" in your play of life like as people? Think of three adjectives you would use to describe each of them, as they were when you were growing up. Their personalities and behavior helped set the tone that influenced your view of how life is, as well as how men and women are or should be. If there was only one parent, where did you look to find models of adults of the other sex, to help you decide how women and men should be?

Dylan and John's story

Dylan and John's mother was creative, energetic, and optimistic. She didn't seem to worry, believing that everything would work out for the best. She had faith that what a person could think of, a person could accomplish. If she was working on a project and someone told her, "You can't do that," she would find another way to accomplish the job.

Dylan's father was a serious, hard-working man who plodded through life providing for his family. His steady (albeit modest) income allowed his wife to become actively involved with "causes" she was passionate about. She worked to improve the local school curriculum, along with heading a committee to insure the continuation of a music program that was slated for budget cuts.

In a workshop Dylan and John attended, they learned about how they had formed their personalities. Dylan realized he had taken a page from his mother's book, concluding that "Life is a place where anything is possible if you're persistent enough." The complaints he had from his girlfriend about how he wouldn't take no for an answer, made sense.

John viewed his family from a different perspective. He realized that his decision had been, "Men have to work to provide, while women get what they want." And he finally understood why, at work, he didn't bother to push an issue with his partner, who was a woman, when they had a disagreement.

The influence of your parents' relationship

What was the interaction between your parents like? Were they both there? Had one abandoned the family, leaving the other to raise you alone? Was one of your parents physically present all the time, while the other was more emotionally present, even if only for short times? Was there a divorce, a separation, or a remarriage in your family? If so, you might have decided that relationships are tenuous or that you can't count on anyone. Perhaps you decided that you will never get married because marriages don't work out. Maybe you believe that it is important to leave a bad or abusive relationship and try again.

If your parents had noisy, abusive, or scary fights, you might see life as a dangerous, stormy place. Did your parents cooperate or compete? Was one parent dominant and the other submissive? Or did they relate as equals, sharing decision-making? If one parent called the shots while the other simply complied, your conclusion might have been that life is a place where there are bosses who make decisions while everyone else falls into line. Did your parents practice mutual respect, talking over decisions and expressing their feelings? Were they warm, loving, and kind to one another or were they cold, angry, and distant? If your parents were engaged in a "cold war," you might expect all relationships to be distant, avoiding them to ward off feelings of isolation. Unless you've had some relationship training, your views on intimacy, cooperation, and negotiation depend largely on how your parents handled their conflicts and differences with each other.

Kelly's story

Kelly was working her way through *Do-It-Yourself Therapy*, developing awareness every week about herself and her relationships.

When she was thinking about the influences of her environment, Kelly recalled her parents' relationship. She remembered how terrified she had felt as a child when her moody, explosive, and angry father yelled at her mother over some minor mistake she'd made, such as a spill or a forgotten chore. Her mother would cower and apologize repeatedly. Other times, her father was mellow and sweet, bringing her mother presents and reading to her on Saturday nights after dinner. She could never count on which father would be coming through the door at night.

Kelly described the atmosphere in her home as "changeable" and "threatening." She realized that her parents' relationship had shaped her beliefs and affected her life in many ways. She had grown up afraid of anger—her own and anyone else's. She feared it would result in the frightening displays she had experienced with her father. She was timid, afraid of taking risks, and fearful of making mistakes, cowering her way through life. She thought men were unpredictable and was careful not to get too close to them.

The influence of parenting styles

In your life, the adults who were responsible for you had a distinct parenting style. It affected how you thought about yourself and how you behaved. Did your parents expect conformity and obedience from children, or were individual differences respected, creativity encouraged, and your opinions appreciated? Did your parents make decisions without consulting you or your siblings, or did they involve you or let you decide for yourself? Did your parents use family meetings to problem solve and share feelings, or were they the kind of parents who thought of children as objects? Did your parents teach you to obey and punish you if you defied them? Did they motivate you to behave as they wanted you to by punishing, hitting, praising, rewarding, or bribing? Did they teach you to think for yourself, even if that meant disagreeing with them? Did they let you do whatever you wanted and wait on you hand and foot? Did they help you have and do what you wanted within limits and expect you to do your part in household tasks?

Maybe your parents disagreed about how to raise you and what the proper discipline should be. It's not unusual that parents disagree. If this happened in your family, you might have decided one of the following: "I know who to ask to get what I want." "I'll just sneak out the back and do what I want while they're busy arguing." "Life is chaotic." "Women are nice but men are mean." Think about how you're still operating on the beliefs you formed in childhood.

Many of the decisions that make up your belief system sprang from your parents' "leadership styles." Although most real-life mothers, fathers, teachers, and caregivers are made up of some combination of the categories we present in the chart on pages 96-97, these four typical parental roles will help you understand the impact adults had on your developing views of self, others, life, and behavior.

Simone's story

Simone's parents were strict authoritarians. From the time she was small, they taught Simone the "correct" way to dress, eat, speak, and behave in public. They made her sit at the table until every bite on her plate was gone and punished her if she didn't. They expected her to do well in school, to study piano, and to play tennis so that she would be well-rounded and well-educated.

Even as a teenager, when she began to express her ideas, their dinner table conversations became a battleground as her father insisted she quote the sources for every idea she supported. He discounted what she had to say if it didn't agree with his own thinking.

Her parents had seen to it that her life was so structured, Simone had neither the time nor the privacy to develop a secret life. She never could experiment with different ways of thinking, feeling, behaving, dressing, or anything else. When Simone went away to college and had to make decisions for herself about what to eat, what to wear, who to hang out with, and whether to do her homework, she was overwhelmed. Within two months she had slept with four men, gained 20 pounds, used five kinds of mind-altering drugs, and withdrew from three of her classes. Before her first semester ended, she was back home in the middle of a severe depression.

The influence of heredity

When you stepped onto the stage of your life, you arrived with certain genetic qualities. These qualities influenced the decisions you made about yourself and may have typecast you.

Many people believe that your temperament or disposition is genetic. However, we would argue that your temperament developed as a result of your unconscious decisions about finding your unique place among your siblings (which we cover later in this week's therapy). Those qualities that are set when you are born rather than formed by your decisions consist of your physical attributes. Are you male or female,

What he or she is called	What he or she believes	What he or she does	What you might decide
The authoritarion parent Autocrat Dictator Commander Ma'am Sir Boss	I am superior. I must be in control. I must be perfect. I am entitled. The child owes me (obedience, gratitude, performance...). I am burdened with responsibilities.	Imposes will through rigid rules. Allows for no flexibility or freedom. Uses pressure and punishment. Demands "respect." Instills fear. Believes there is only one right way. Ignores feelings. Treats child like a possession instead of a person. Demands obedience and issues orders. Imposes ideas. Dominates. Depends on criticism and praise to control. Rewards, bribes, threatens, and punishes. Lectures. Yells. Nags. Takes all responsibility. Makes all decisions. Overprotects. Pities child. Acts self-righteous. Spoils or shames child. Is overconcerned with fairness. Gives with strings attached. Demands perfection and finds fault. Overconcerned about what others think.	I am powerless, out of control. I depend on others (men/women). I am not responsible. I am not a good as.... No one can tell me what to do. I better conform. Other people know better than I do. I can't think for myself. Power is important. I must win or be right. I must hide my true feelings. I'll get even. I give up. I'll be "good" so I won't get "caught." I behave when others make me. I'll sneak to do/get what I want. I'm inadequate. I need to be superior to others. Others take advantage of me. I'm never good enough. I must be perfect. Others protect and decide for me.
The permissive parent Marshmallow Wimp Pushover Easy Rug	I don't count. Others are more important than I am. I am powerless, out of control. I have no rights. The child has all the rights.	Gives all power to child. Provides no rules, structure, or limits. Overindulges child. Wants to shelter child from every uncomfortable feeling. Gives child all responsibility for decisions. Becomes a slave. Gives in to demands. Feels guilty about saying "no." Coaxes. Begs. Is kind but not firm. Allows plenty of freedom but without any order. Respects child but not self.	Others will give me things and take care of me. I expect to receive. The world revolves around me. I am the one who calls the shots. I have a right to do exactly as I wish. There are no limits. Life is not safe. I am unloved. I depend on others to meet my needs and give me what I want.

What he or she is called	What he or she believes	What he or she does	What you might decide
The neglectful parent Absent Sick or addicted	I should be a better parent. I don't know how to do my job. I'd rather be partying. My kid is a pest. Leave me alone. I hate this.	Makes no demands, recognizes no demands. Is neither firm nor kind. Provides neither freedom nor limits. Respects neither self nor child.	I'm not important. I'm not loved or lovable. I'm unworthy. No one cares about me. I'll have to decide everything for myself. I have to take care of myself. I'm not worth taking care of, even by myself.
The firm and kind parent Leader Guide Coach Friend Mentor	The child can make decisions. I am equal, not more or less worthwhile than others. I am human and have the courage to be imperfect. Mistakes are opportunities to learn. All people are important, including me. I am in charge but can be flexible. I trust myself and my child.	Shares power. Leads with kindness and firmness. Treats others with respect. Treats child as responsible, worthwhile human being. Encourages child to make decisions. Lets child be who he or she is. Encourages independence. Gives choices. Expects child to contribute. Promotes equality. Avoids making child feel guilt. Sets realistic standards. Is not concerned with own image. Knows when to say no. Invites, asks, requests. Persuades, exercises influence, wins cooperation. Listens to child's ideas. Encourages child to do better and helps child to improve. Speaks in friendly voice. Shows faith. Focuses on strengths. Listens and shares feelings. Uses routines to create order. Acknowledges effort, not just achievement. Focuses on process of learning. Shares responsibility. Teaches child self-discipline.	I am responsible, respectful toward others, self-disciplined, self-determining. I can cooperate with others. Others include me in deciding. I can think for myself. I am capable. I am open to others' ideas. I count, am important. I can solve problems. I can rely on myself. I am good enough and a valuable person as I am. I can trust others. Mistakes are for learning. I don't have to be perfect. I can try new experiences.

tall or short, stocky or angular? What color are your eyes, your hair, your skin? What is your bone structure? What sound does your voice make? What kind of vision do you have? How's your hearing?

You made decisions about what you could and couldn't do based, at least in part, on what you noticed about yourself. For example, if you entered with one of your feet on backwards, you had to decide what to do with that. You could spend your life sitting, waiting for others to come to you and do for you. Or you could hop around after your siblings and insist they include you in their games.

If you are short, you could decide you weren't as good as those who were tall, expect not to be noticed, and keep to yourself, or you could make sure you raised a ruckus every time you wanted to be recognized. If you were born with what you saw as a face "only a mother could love," you could decide you'd have to develop your personality or your intellect to compensate. Or, you could decide not to expect much attention and appreciation in life since you didn't have the good looks to earn it. Or, you may choose reconstructive surgery to achieve the look you want (with today's technology, there's very little about the body that cannot be altered).

Ben's story

Ben, an active five year old, contracted polio and spent many months in an iron lung, watching life pass by. Although he recovered enough to walk on crutches and leave the confines of the iron lung, he never got his carefree attitude back.

His parents wanted him to experience a normal life, so they sent him to the local public school, where Ben felt awkward and out of place and hid out in the back of the classroom, hoping he wouldn't be noticed. He developed a rich inner life, including a love of music and art.

The fear of isolation and helplessness that he experienced in the iron lung hung over him like a ghost, so he made sure he always dated women who could look after him. In many ways, he limited his ability to do for himself by choosing a partner who was a caregiver, who felt sorry for him, and thought he needed more help than he did.

The influence of your siblings

Every play needs conflict to keep the audience captivated. What better way is there to provide conflict than to add more players (or, in your case, siblings). More than any other single factor, your personality was formed by the decisions you made interacting with your siblings and your view from your birth order position. Think about how it was for you as you read Mary's, Mason's, and Minnie's stories. Each child is born into a somewhat different familiar atmosphere, because parents and the way they parent changes over time as they gain age and experience. The stresses acting on the family also ebb and flow with job changes, moving, death, and divorce, as well as the birth of additional children. Pay special attention to how Mary, Mason, and Minnie improvised. Ask yourself if you used any of these methods when you were pushed out onto the stage of your life.

Mary's story: the first born

When Mary was born, there were two adults working and taking care of the household. They seemed busy and happy to be with each other, eager for Mary's arrival...as well as being anxious and tense. One said, "I know we'll be perfect parents." The other said, "This is such a big responsibility! The right food, the right clothes, the right pediatrician, the right schools...." The first parent replied, "Don't worry. We have it under control. We'll know all the answers by the time he needs them," to which the other replied, "You mean, by the time she needs them."

From the day of Mary's birth, all the action focused on her. She heard them say, "We're so happy you're here. You're incredible and perfect." The adults watched everything Mary did, and then reported her behaviors to the rest of the family. When Mary cried, one of her parents was there immediately. Mary's parents were many times her size, moved swiftly, seemed sure of themselves, knew what to do, and seemed to understand what she needed. The adults appeared efficient and capable. What do you think Mary might have been deciding? What would you have decided? How about, "I'm important. I'm the center of the universe. I'm small. I can depend on others to meet needs. Life is tense but predictable."

Most of the time Mary was quiet and contented, but on occasion she would notice frowns on the adults' faces. What do you think she might have been thinking then? What would you have thought? Could it be, "They only love me when I'm good. I'd better not make a mess. I have to figure out how to please them."

Mary's parents were serious about their job of parenting, intensely focused on Mary and they determined to do everything right. As Mary grew, she copied the big people in her world, attempting to please them, do things the right way, the perfect way—the way big people did. She often heard the adults say, "She's such an easy, happy baby. She learns so quickly. She's so good, she doesn't give us any trouble. She does just what we ask!" Perhaps she decided, "I don't give anyone trouble. I'm smart. I can do what they do."

Mary might be well on her way to growing up to be a responsible leader; she was diligent and serious, conforming to the rules and values of the family, or of "authority." This is true of a lot of first borns, and probably happened with you if you were a first born. It makes sense, given the typical influences you encountered at birth. Little did you or Mary know that the play was about to take an unexpected turn which would affect your views of yourself, others, and life forever.

Mason's story: the second born

When Mason entered in the second act, he came into a different world than Mary, who had entered a childless world and set the standard for how children should be. When Mason came on stage, the second-born, it appeared as though everyone else had read the script. Mason had to improvise for a while, figuring out the setting, plot, and characters. He saw two adults focused their adoration on a cute, smart, well-behaved three-year-old girl at center stage. She looked big compared to Mason. He saw how clever and skillful she already was with using the toilet, eating with a spoon, pouring cereal, and singing songs.

He noticed that the adults were busy, but they seemed relaxed and confident. They were calmer and more experienced in their roles as parents than they were when their first child was born. Mason was already making some decisions about what he saw: "I'm little; others are big. Sister is clever, quick, and quiet. Life is calm."

After Mason burst on stage, the focus of attention shifted to him. He tried out interactions with each of the others and watched carefully to see what unfolded. He observed that when he made noises others noticed him. He decided, "Noise gets noticed. If I'm quiet no one looks."

Meanwhile Mary was deciding, as she noticed how the adults treated newborn Mason, that "I'm not helpless or fussy like him. I'll have to be really good for them to like me now." She may have believed that her special place was threatened, and felt upstaged or "dethroned" by the enthralling little novelty of her baby brother. She had to figure out how she could stay in the spotlight she had grown used to; how she could stay first, ahead of Mason. How did your first-born sibling stay ahead of you? How did you behave to find your special place in the limelight?

One day, Mason's mother was busy putting laundry in the dryer and didn't come when he cried out. He cried louder and finally she bustled into the room looking harried, her brow creased. He decided, "I'm annoying. I have to scream to be heard. She doesn't have time for me. I'm not important." As his mother changed his diaper, Mason's big sister Mary brought his bottle, and he heard his mother say, "What a big girl and a great helper you are to notice your baby brother is hungry. He was crying so hard. He's not quiet like you." When Mary heard the comparison, she enjoyed the recognition, it also felt like an overwhelming pressure. Mason decided, "Sister's responsible. I'm little. She's quiet. I'm loud."

Later Mason saw Mary playing with blocks. He crawled over to explore and knocked over the pile she was making. She pushed him away and he cried out. His sister said, "You broke my building. You're not supposed to play like that; don't you know anything?!" Mother came and scolded Mason, picked him up, and he cried harder. Mother then put Mason in his bed, saying, "You just sit in there and think about what you did! No treat for you this afternoon!" Mason decided, "I wreck things. I mess things up. Mother takes care of me when I cry. Girls are skilled and bossy. I don't play right. Mom makes a fuss when I'm naughty." There are countless "stage directions," characterizations, and dialogue both Mary and Mason might be writing into their personal versions of the script which they make up as they go through life. As the action unfolds around them, they determine the meaning and improvise their part in each interaction. You did the same thing when you were a child. Can you remember some of your decisions?

If you're a second-born like Mason, you may not be concerned with following the rules and meeting adult expectations, or even recognizing the rules, as first-born Mary did. You arrived in an environment that was more relaxed, because your "practiced" parents were calmer and less strict in their parental roles. Reflecting that atmosphere, you may have become flexible and friendly.

Like every child born, you searched for a way to create your own place, and to be unique and special in your family. You had the mistaken belief of every child, "I have to be different from the others to be special and stand out, or my parents won't love me." And you chose your different way of being unconsciously. First children believe they must be first, while second children try harder to catch up. Your parents were probably astonished by how different their children were. The areas you picked to compete in and where you chose to distinguish yourselves from each other are likely to have been those areas which were part of your family's values.

It's not unusual to find one child conforming, embracing, and adopting a parent's approach to a certain issue, while another rebels. This happens whether parents agree or disagree about the issue.

Often, a second born will look at an accomplished older child and conclude "That's the way to belong," and then set out to catch up to or out do his or her older sibling. This often happens if the two are close in age or the same sex. If this is what happened in your case, maybe the oldest child in your family switched roles. When a child becomes discouraged, sometimes he or she thinks that, "If I can't be first by being the best, I'll be first by being the worst."

Minnie's story: the last born

When Minnie, the youngest child came onto the stage, everything changed. It seemed to the parents that their older children had grown a foot over night. All of a sudden they looked so much bigger and more capable than before Minnie arrived. Mason and Mary now became part of the support staff. They could soothe and entertain themselves, fetch items needed for the baby, help out Mom and Dad, and be caretakers in a pinch.

Mary, now five years old, was already thinking, "I know what to do." Defending her title as "the helpful, mature, and responsible one," Mary was comfortable in the role of "little mother." She helped feed Minnie, play with her, dress her, boss her around, and do all the things Minnie was too little to handle. Minnie might have decided as the youngest, "I'm the smallest. Everyone is bigger than I am. I might trip and fall. Others carry me. Others will take care of me. Life is a breeze."

What Minnie saw was a stage filled with action. Her mother and father were sometimes short with each other. There was always too much to do, they disagreed about who should do what, and sometimes they fought. Minnie had to figure out how to fit in and get noticed. So, she smiled, cooed, babbled, and laughed. Everyone responded warmly when she made funny little noises and cute little faces. Minnie's family members told her she was adorable and spent time playing with her. No matter how busy, there was always someone who could see to her needs. She just had to figure out whether she would catch up with brother and sister and do what they did, or sit back and let them come to her.

One day as Minnie tried to tie her shoe for the first time, Mason rushed over saying, "Here, Minnie, I'll do that for you." Minnie decided, "I can't do it. I'm incapable." If Mom, Dad, Mason, and Mary continued to give Minnie attention every time she needed something, she would grow up with little confidence and a sense of entitlement. This often happens with the youngest child. If there's always someone bigger, older, stronger, and quicker doing for them what they might be struggling to learn for themselves, youngest children conclude they can never measure up and never catch up, so why try. Did you make decisions like these if you are the youngest in your family?

As Minnie grew, she watched her big sister Mary go off to school. Mary didn't have many friends, but she focused her energy on achieving academic honors. She decided early on that she wanted to be a lawyer. Minnie decided that the "good student" place in the family was already taken, and proceeded to do more of what she was good at— socializing. She socialized so much in her family that she distinguished herself as the "social, gregarious one."

Teachers often called Minnie "Chatty Cathy" because she spent class time talking to her friends, instead of paying attention to the lesson. The phone was always ringing at home, where she spent hours visiting with her friends. Her mother and father described her as their "social butterfly." What did your parents say about you?

Unless your parents made a point of encouraging your independence, you may have stayed the "baby" and had fewer opportunities to learn skills. If you were clever at getting others to do for you, maybe you make a great committee head today! As the youngest, maybe you're cute, charming, and playful, but you frequently complain that you're not taken seriously. However, you might have the highest sociability rating of any of your siblings.

Mason becomes the middle child

Where Mason once had the distinction of being the smallest, newest, cutest, and most challenging member of his family, he was now unseated. Someone new had taken over that spot. He found himself in a dilemma. Who was he and how would he distinguish himself since charming little Minnie had arrived? Would "loudmouth, irresponsible, mess maker" be enough to keep him visible in the growing throng?

Often a middle child feels squeezed, having neither the privileges of the oldest nor the freedom of the youngest child. If you're a middle child you might have developed a special talent to distinguish yourself. Or, you might have felt crowded out, unsure of your position. You probably had some doubts about how you'd continue to receive the family's attention.

The motto of the middle child is, "Life is unfair." Being in the middle, you see both sides, so you may have been sensitive to justice and fairness. It's a belief that can make you give up or mount a campaign to right injustice. Were you a mediator in your family (are you one now)? When you're discouraged, you may express concern with justice by harboring bitterness or by seeking revenge. As a child, you saw children who were smaller and younger and less skillful than you. You also saw children who were bigger, older, and probably more skilled than you. You had a broader range of models and characteristics to compare yourself with than either your oldest or youngest sibling.

Mason was only two when Minnie entered the scene. Mason's parents were disturbed when he became "louder," often crying and fussing. Nothing they did seemed to comfort him. From the beginning he seemed "difficult," and he seemed to be getting worse. He was allergic to milk, didn't eat the same food his family ate, and was still wetting his bed at the age of six. While Mary picked up her toys when asked, Mother had to tell Mason again and again. Mary was so helpful, she sometimes jumped in to pick the toys up for him.

Mother often asked Mason why he couldn't be more like his sister. Mason usually replied with a wordless shrug. When Mason went to school, teachers said, "Oh, you're Mary's brother, I'm so happy you're in my class," until they got to know him. He often tuned out in class, staring out the window, sketching furiously in his notebook. Mason had decided there was room for only one "student" in the family. Mason brought his notebook home to show his parents. They were impressed with his detailed drawings, as well as the concentration and imagination he showed. However, they disapproved of his macabre themes of death, killing, and war—they found them disturbing. They took him to a psychiatrist, believing him to be troubled.

Minnie enjoyed lying on the floor in Mason's room, drawing on her little pad with her crayons while he sketched. One day Mason's mother noticed them together and took Minnie by the hand, concerned about the influence her rebellious son would have on his little sister. "You're not the artist type," she asserted. "Why don't you come play a game with me?"

Silently, she despaired for her son. She wished he would find more valuable things to do with his time than isolate himself with a sketch book, drawing what looked like storyboards for horror films. Although she didn't say it aloud, he saw her disapproving messages through her body language and facial expressions. "Artist," he thinks. "So that's what I am...messy...loner...moody...."

As a teenager, Mason wrecked the family car, abused drugs, and hung out with kids who got in trouble. His parents threatened and punished him, made rules he didn't follow—they even made plans to send him to a boarding school. Mason created his place in the family and in school as "the difficult one." It distinguished him from his sisters, giving him a big share of his parents' and teachers' energy and attention, even if it worked in a negative way.

Now that the story line was written for each child, the adults unwittingly did their part to reinforce the decisions each child was making. Although the children's decisions weren't conscious, they shaped their personalities as they worked to define each of their roles in life. What character did you create for yourself in your play of life?

Dan's story: an only child

If you're an only child, you may be wondering, "What about me? I didn't have siblings to help form my personality!" Maybe you will relate to Dan's story.

When Dan crawled upon the stage of life, he joined a couple who had waited until their mid-thirties to become parents. He was their first child, and would be their last. His father was a well-established attorney, and his mother had just quit her advertising job to be home with Dan full-time. He was the only grandchild, and his every tooth, step, smile, word, and deed was captured in albums, on video tape, and in scrapbooks. Mother did most everything for him, including the cooking, housekeeping, laundry, packing his school lunch, and hanging up his clothes. He loved to watch sports on television with his dad. As he grew up, he pursued basketball, baseball, karate, tennis, and fencing. His parents had the money to buy the equipment, his mother had the time to drive him around to practices and games, and both parents had time to attend his matches. His trophies lined the shelves of the family room.

What do you think Dan decided? What would you decide in the same circumstances? "I can do/have whatever I want. I'm the most important person in the world to others. I get all the attention. Others do for me. Life will provide. Life is orderly and safe."

If you were an only child, like a first born, you entered an adults-only world. But like a last-born, you were never dethroned by a new sibling. You had your own space and your own possessions, so you may find it difficult to share or to not have things your own way. If you decided that the road to belonging was paved with adult behavior, you may have become super responsible, achievement oriented, independent, self-sufficient, and set high standards for yourself, like eldest children tend to do. But because there were no siblings competing for your parents' attention and family resources, you may have gotten used to being the center of attention. If, like many youngest children, you had everything done for you, you may not have developed skills for independence. You might have felt incompetent, comparing yourself to the capable grown-ups around you. In your discouragement you might have decided you were helpless and dependent. What you decided depends largely on how your parents treated you, since there were no siblings to help you fit into the family and the world. The motto of the only child is "I'm the one and only and I'm special."

When children come of age

In your adulthood, many of the beliefs you formed early on still serve you well. They lead you to success, to meet the requirements of any situation. Yet, at other times those same decisions may create problems for you. You may be missing out on options you don't realize you have. This happens if you take the beliefs you formed in childhood to the extreme or think in terms of absolutes.

What would happen if Dan, accustomed to being the one and only important person, grew up and married Minnie, who was the family social butterfly? He probably would end up unhappy, looking for ways to feel special. Perhaps he'd spend a lot of time playing sports as a way of maintaining his uniqueness and sense of belonging. And what would Minnie do if he complained about her being too social? She would probably feel unloved and misunderstood, and spend more time with people who enjoyed her as she was.

Imagine Minnie growing up and having children. She'd be playful and childlike, but might have a difficult time keeping up with the household chores and other responsibilities of parenthood. She could hire a housekeeper if she could afford to, or hope her husband would take care of her and the children. Without someone looking out for her, she would feel both overwhelmed and resentful. Minnie might look for places where her social skills could be appreciated, heading up committees and fund raisers.

Or, what would happen to Mason as an adult? He could end up in jail and become an addict, or he could find an outlet for his artistic gifts. He would need to realize that his problem behaviors were a response to his need to find a special place for himself in the family and not some deep-seated psychological disturbance.

Mary, who eventually became an attorney, was used to pressure and juggling a lot of balls at one time. She was able to approach her anxious clients and the paralegals who assisted her with the same confident attitude she'd learned as a child playing "mother" to her younger siblings. Yet, some situations were inexplicably upsetting to cool, capable Mary. When the pressure was on to learn something new, she felt anxious and lost sleep. She was angry having to add a skill to her repertoire and she worried that she wouldn't be good enough to pass the test. If Mary didn't think she was first in her field, she would work relentlessly to keep the spot she had forged for herself. She feared a loss of prestige and love if she didn't measure up to her own high standards. This set her apart from her colleagues, who found Mary to be standoffish and unfriendly. They didn't enjoy spending time with her away from work, not that Mary had much time to play.

Do you identify with the adults in our scenarios? Did the decisions you made as a child help you or hurt you as an adult? Do you know that you can change your decisions now?

Variations on the theme

If you found that the description of others of your same birth order don't fit very well for you, it's because you gave your own unique meanings to what and who surrounded you in your early years. No two eldest children are exactly the same, nor are two middles or two youngest.

If you are a first born, pursued and passed up by a second born, you may have become discouraged, giving up the place of responsible achiever to your younger sibling. Perhaps the typical characteristics of a second or middle child suit you better.

You may be a middle child and identify with the characteristics of a first born or the youngest in the family. If you came from a large family with large gaps between children, or from a blended family, your family may have included several different "constellations." While only one child was the chronological eldest, perhaps the oldest of a second group of children coming three or four years after the birth of the youngest, has the characteristics of a typical first born (what we would call a "psychological eldest"). Large age gaps could also have created the influences of an only or youngest child position for one of you who was born somewhere in the middle.

The invitation to stay dependent upon overprotective parents and siblings can be refused. Many youngest children decide to run as fast as they can to catch up with "the big kids," insisting on doing things for themselves, growing up to be dynamic go-getters. Maybe you're a youngest child who was given opportunities to learn skills and were expected to participate, so that you developed self-reliance and grew up to be responsible and capable.

When examining your birth order's influence on your personality, it's important not to leave out children who died in childhood, stillborn children, or even miscarriages. Parents often react to a death or miscarriage by being extremely protective of their surviving children. Their attitude impacts your decisions about yourself and life. In the process of deciding whether and how you can be "good enough," you might find it impossible to compete with a ghost for a sibling.

The possible conclusions each child can make are limitless. Each of us is unique. It's this creative ability that accounts for the incredible variety we experience among human beings. The "family pie" exercise in the **Activities** section at the end of this chapter will help you clarify how you interpreted your birth order position and decided that you are special. It will help you recognize how your birth order is still part of who you are and how you relate to others.

Living in awareness and acceptance

Now that you're aware of some of the influences of your childhood decisions about yourself, others, and life, you may be discovering what some of those decisions were. You might be thinking, "What a jerk I've been!" or "How stupid I am," or maybe, "What's the problem with that?" and pass instant judgment on yourself or your "traits." It is important to remember that when you adopted these convictions, you were a child trying to figure out how to belong in your family and how to be special. Considering your lack of life experience and perspective, it's inevitable that you would make some mistakes. Those decisions, even ones that now seem erroneous, helped you to get through childhood.

If you grew up in an abusive situation it was probably wise "not to make any waves." However, not expressing any complaints could invite problems for you in relationships today. With an adult perspective, you can develop empathy and compassion for that "little child"; your child within you did the best he or she could. As you examine which decisions are helpful to you in your life today (and which are inviting problems) don't be too quick to rewrite them. As you increase your awareness, remember to work on self-acceptance. Acceptance means knowing that you're a worthwhile human being, in spite of your faults. With acceptance, you can look at how being special brings you successes...and any subsequent difficulties. Acceptance means recognizing the reality of what is. Without acceptance, true change isn't possible.

 ## Creating changes in your world

By taking small steps, you can develop your awareness of what you decided during your crucial first years on life's stage. **Obstacles to Growth and Change** will help you identify where you may be stuck, and **Easy Steps for Change** will show you how to practice increasing your awareness and acceptance of how you shaped your personality. The **Activities** section contains more opportunities to discover options for changing the beliefs you'd like to modify.

Obstacles to growth and change

1. If you're still comparing yourself to your siblings, instead of appreciating the differences between you, you may be focusing on how much better or worse they're doing and this will keep you feeling pressured and discouraged.

2. If you blame your parents or your siblings for who you are or the difficulties that you have, you'll stay helpless and stuck.

3. If you're aware of the decisions you made about how to be special, but have judgments about those decisions, it will be difficult to make and maintain changes.

4. If you see yourself or others as a victims of heredity, you'll be stuck in "poor me" thinking and nothing will change.

5. If you limit your interests or efforts because you think all the good "parts" are taken, you'll be missing out on experience and depriving yourself of choices.

6. If you are letting others define who you are, stereotyping you as "the baby," "lazy," "jokester," and so forth, you may be stopping yourself from participating in life fully.

7. You won't achieve self-acceptance if you set conditions such as "only if" or "as long as" on who you are. Examples: I'm okay as long as I take care of everyone else. I count only if I'm funny and friendly. I know I am someone as long as I'm difficult.

Easy steps for change

☑ Write down three adjectives to describe yourself as a child. Practice saying, "I am (your adjectives)" and see how true those statements are today. Give yourself permission to be who you are. Look for ways those qualities are helpful to you. Now look for ways they may be limiting you.

☑ Write down a quality you think only your sibling has and then look to see if you have that quality as well.

☑ If you have a negative or limited view of one of your siblings, think of some way to expand your understanding of him or her.

☑ Find a picture of yourself as a young child (or draw one), put it in a place where you spend time. Tell the child something encouraging each day.

☑ Write: I am the (fill in your birth order) child in my family. The advantages of that position are _____. The disadvantages of that position are _____.

☑ Draw a picture of the family you grew up in and give it a title. What would each of the people in the drawing say if each could speak? What do you learn about yourself when you look at the drawing?

☑ Write as many traits as you can think of that attracted you to your current intimate partner. Turn the paper over and write the names of each of your siblings and some adjectives that would describe them as you remember them when you were a child. Look back at the list you have on the other side of the paper and see which "sibling" you partnered with.

☑ Take five minutes and write a list of your strengths and abilities. Read the list out loud.

☑ Now write a list of what you think are your weaknesses. Read this list aloud, and after each item add the phrase "...and I accept this as part of me."

Activities

1. To learn more about what you decided your unique place in your family was, draw a circle and divide it into the number of slices that correspond to how many children were in your

family. Don't forget to leave a space for any children who died, as they are also part of your identity. Write the name of one child (including yourself) in each slice of the pie. By each child's name, write how much older or younger she/he is than you (Billy +3, Sue -2). Now, write three or four adjectives that describe each child as he or she was growing up. Look at your pie and notice how you decided each person was different and special. The adjectives in your own piece of the pie are beliefs about yourself: "I am...". Who was most different from you? In what ways? Who was most like you? In what ways? Here are more of your beliefs about "I am...". How do your answers impact your current situation?

2. Do you notice yourself judging the decisions you made about how you were special? Do you hear an inner voice defending the adjectives you came up with for yourself? Is the voice explaining, protecting, comparing, or limiting? This is your internal critic at work. To learn to accept yourself, pick a statement from the list below that fits, or make up your own.

   ☑ It's okay to be different from my siblings.

   ☑ Isn't it interesting that I still see myself like this?

   ☑ I have a hard time accepting some of my qualities.

   ☑ Because I wrote a quality for a sibling doesn't mean it can't apply to me as well.

   ☑ I don't have to limit my view of myself.

   ☑ I accept myself in spite of my faults and imperfections.

   ☑ <u>(make up your own)</u>.

3. It is time to create your script for your play of life. This activity takes some time, but it is worthwhile to write out all the answers and keep the information to look at again. Each time you look at your script, you'll learn more about yourself, how you think, and what you do as a result of your decisions. You can also use this information to make changes using the suggestions you'll find in Week 5, where we talk about rewriting your beliefs.

   A. Write a story that starts with, "When I was a child, I grew up in a place where..." Read your story and write down three influences that this setting has on your life today.

B. Describe the atmosphere in your family. How did it influence the person you are today? Did the atmosphere change over time? Does it impact the person you are today?

C. What were your family's values about money, religion, relationships, or anything else? Did you accept each value or rebel against it? How did your family values shape your life today?

D. Write three adjectives to describe each of the adult caregivers in your family when you were a child. How did their personalities impact your life?

E. What decisions have you made about relationships, based on how the adults in your life interacted?

F. List the genetic qualities you brought with you to your play of life and comment on how they have influenced your decisions about yourself.

G. Look at the Parenting Styles Chart on pages 96-97 and see if you can identify the primary parenting style in the family where you grew up. How was your personality influenced by the style in which you were parented? Use the chart to help you out.

If you are in a relationship, it might be interesting to have your partner do this same activity. Compare your notes, looking for places where your plays are similar, places where they are different, and potential spots for conflict.

 **Week 5**

Put Your Childhood Memories to Work

Why look back at your childhood to move forward? When we first introduce the idea of early memories in the therapy process, we often hear, "But I don't remember anything from my childhood." "I don't have any good memories." "Do I have to think of a negative memory?" "I don't want to remember my past." "I've put the past behind me and that's where it should stay." "What do my childhood memories have to do with getting help on my procrastinating?" If any of this sounds familiar, **please do not skip your therapy this week!** You will miss out on discovering the hidden treasure of your lifetime.

You have all the information you need inside of you to do your own therapy. What we have found is that most of our clients have that information, but they don't know how to access it. Work with early memories gives our clients a key to unlock that treasure chest within, uncovering the valuable knowledge hidden from their awareness. Some people regard this as work only to be done within the confines of an expert's office. We believe that you can handle using this information to facilitate your own therapy. The more you work on your childhood memories, the better you will know yourself.

As you uncover the treasures hidden in your memory, you'll discover your worldview and your core beliefs. We call these beliefs your private logic. (We use terms such as unconscious beliefs, private logic, separate realities, belief system, and lifestyle interchangeably in our work.) Your memories are selective, meaning that you only remember those which fit your own private logic. Using your memories, you can learn more about where your patterns of thinking, feeling, and behaving originated and pinpoint what you need to work on. You'll meet your inner child, who is waiting for your adult self to honor, comfort, parent, and help him or her grow up. Memory work is a method where you can learn about your hidden history and put together your personal story. Lurking in your childhood memories is some either/or thinking that has stopped you from moving forward. By examining your early memories, you can find the moment your self-esteem was damaged and you decided the person you are wasn't good enough. Your early memories will even show you what you decided you had to do to be worthwhile.

Don't be surprised if you uncover some secrets that have been making you sick, or have tried to get your attention. Be reassured that whatever pain surfaces won't stay for long if you allow yourself to listen to what your memories are telling you. We'll show you how to keep yourself safe and we'll help you move through your pain, instead of dragging it along with you forever. Memory work does bring old wounds to the surface. However, you can work on past issues that were buried, but have not disappeared. Then you can heal. You will learn how to interpret body memories, those childhood memories that generate a physical reaction in your body. Some of these memories were created before you acquired verbal language.

Early memory work is optimistic, interesting, and exciting. The focus is not on what happened, but on what, as a young child, you decided about what happened. Today, as an adult with awareness, you can make new decisions that can change your life. By calling on your inner child as a consultant, you'll discover that although you didn't have a lot of control over what happened, you can now control how your past experiences affect you today. Our clients are usually delighted to find that their personalities aren't genetic and their conditions haven't left them permanently damaged. They realize they aren't stuck for the rest of their lives with feelings of depression, sadness, or exhaustion. They find that the suicidal tendencies, addictions, or other conditions they believed to be inherited may be based on an early subconscious decision and are not a lifelong sentence.

Did your memories really happen?

There is a lot of controversy about false memories, and in the course of the discussions, many people have become afraid of working with early memories. Be wary of others' attempts to give you memories, change your memories, or decide what your memories mean. Only you can do that.

It is possible that some of your memories are a collection of images from real events that are mixed together to form one memory. For example, you might recall a violent confrontation taking place in a location other than the one where it happened, if there was violence in your life and you did visit that location on some occasion. Or, if you and your family members participated in the same event, your memories could sound different from theirs because of their different perspectives. Your memory might be that you walked for miles to get to the store, while your parent remembers the same store as being at the end of the block.

Some of your memories may seem unclear to you. This doesn't mean they didn't happen. It could be that you disregarded certain details that didn't match with what you'd already decided about life, yourself, or others. It could mean that the event was so traumatic you blocked out parts of it. If you were sexually abused as a young child, the abuse could have happened before you knew words like "intercourse," "genitalia," or "sex." Or you might remember a parent as being very sick or sleeping because you didn't know words like "drunk" or "alcoholic."

All of your memories are part of the fabric that makes you the person you are today. As you work on your therapy this week, your memories will show you what makes you unique. You will also learn how to use your childhood memories as aides to change your thoughts, feelings, or actions to heal the past or get unstuck and move forward.

How to do early memory work

You can work on one memory or multiple memories to get the information you need. If you are struggling with a school problem, love issue, parenting dilemma, money matters, work or friendship concerns, and so forth, first think about the issue. Then pretend your life is on a film reel and let your mind roll back to a specific day, moment, or event in your childhood. Don't censor your memories or search for the one that seems to fit the problem. The first memory that comes to your mind, no matter how unrelated it seems, will be exactly the one you need.

If you are drawing a blank, think about where you lived as a child and who you lived with—then see what surfaces. If you're still stuck, use a story that was told about you or describe a photograph that pops into mind. Try a recent memory, even if it only happened last week. If all else fails, make one up. Amazingly, we have found that this is beneficial for our clients; you cannot make up something that doesn't fit with your private logic.

Earlene's memory

"I found my pet cat in the yard and he was dead. I ran to tell my mother, but she was on the phone. She put me off and I became hysterical. I was seven years old, and my seven-year-old inner child was deciding, 'My mom's friends are more important than me. My mom doesn't take me seriously.'"

Nell's memory

"I found a coin on the playground and quickly put it in my pocket without seeing it clearly. I told myself, 'I'll examine it later in private.' I lost the coin as I was getting on the school bus but I didn't notice until I sat down. Another kid found the coin and gave it to the bus driver who asked, 'Did anyone lose some money?' I said I'd lost a coin, but when he asked what it was, I didn't know if it was a quarter or a 50-cent piece. I was sure it was mine. The bus driver said, 'Yeah, right.' I never got the coin. I felt embarrassed and angry. My eight-year-old inner child decided that I was stupid and should know the difference between a quarter and a 50-cent piece."

Discovering your core beliefs

Like you, people experience life, and then made decisions about what was happening. These decisions were crucial in helping each of them understand how they fit in, how they saw others, how life worked and what they thought they needed to do to survive. Their memories, like yours, are both the containers and mirrors for the subconscious decisions made in

Hint   A specific focus brings forth a specific memory

When you are looking for a memory, make sure you focus on one time in particular, instead of a situation that frequently happened. Write out the memory exactly as you recall it, and include all the details. Don't worry if someone once told you it didn't happen that way—what is important is how *you* remember it. Now write down the feeling you have in the memory, your age at the time, and what your inner child was thinking or deciding when the memory happened. Your inner child is you in the memory.

those early years. And like you, the people who shared their memories did more than make decisions. They began looking at their lives, collecting proof that what they decided was true. If an experience didn't fit their belief system, they either didn't notice it, forgot it, or twisted it around to match their view of the world.

To discover your early decisions, ask yourself, "What was my inner child thinking?" The age you are in the memory is the age you were when you made your decisions. Earlene's decision is an example, "My mom's friends are more important than me and my mom doesn't take me seriously."

Earlene, age 40, was working on a project with a colleague at her graphic arts company. The colleague asked Earlene to do him a favor. Instead of telling him she was busy and needed time to think, she yelled at him in an abusive manner until he backed off from asking her for help. Later, Earlene apologized for her behavior and said, "I don't know what got into me. I guess I didn't think you were listening to me or taking me seriously, and it really upset me. Come to think of it, I feel that way a lot."

Earlene's colleague reached out and gave her arm a playful squeeze. "You know I take you seriously and really like working with you, but I'd probably have an easier time listening to you if you didn't bite my head off." It is difficult for Earlene to handle this situation differently, because when she believes others aren't taking her seriously, the seven-year-old who lives inside her acts out. Resorting to the same skills she had at age seven, 40-year-old Earlene screams and attacks.

Earlene isn't aware that she is acting like a 7 year old when she yells at others. Doing the early memory work helped Earlene uncover this information. She felt embarrassed at first, but then she realized that she couldn't do anything about what she didn't recognize was a problem. Now that she understands herself better, she can sit her seven-year-old inner child on her lap and tell her, "You were really hurt and angry and scared when your cat died, and you needed someone to help you deal with the situation. I'm sorry it was so hard for you. When you get scared, I'll be there to help you. I know we can work it out together." Her behavior began to change after that.

Another way to uncover core beliefs is to ask a group of friends to listen to your memory and then to make guesses as to what they think you decided about yourself or others. Their ideas aren't right or wrong, but rather their separate realities viewing your separate reality. Ask your friends to brainstorm their thoughts and write them down. Then you can look at the list and underline the beliefs that fit for you.

Nell's decisions

Here's how Nell's friends interpreted her memory about the coin. They put a big sheet of paper on the wall, then drew four columns on the paper titled "I," "Others," "Life," and "Therefore," as shown on the next page. The "Therefore" column shows the decisions a person made on how to act in order to belong and be significant.

After the group brainstormed what they thought Nell's core beliefs might be, Nell was asked to underline any of the choices that matched how she saw herself, others, and life in that moment. Nell grabbed a marker, and without giving it a second thought, underlined, "I should know better" and "I take my time with things" in the first column; she thought for a moment and then marked "Others stop me from having what's mine" in the second column and "Life is a place where you don't get what you're entitled to" from the third column. From the fourth column she chose, "Therefore, I wait." She looked at her friends and said, "This is the story of my life right now. I have so much to work on, I don't feel like I'm getting anywhere, I'm not sure I'm in the right job, and I don't feel happy in my marriage. Did I leave anything out?"

Nell took the list home and wrote down the items she'd underlined on a small slip of paper, which she kept in her day planner. Whenever she had a spare minute, she looked at her list. She noticed that her decisions were powerful. They seemed to her more like objective truth than her own separate reality. She kept struggling with the notion that she "created" these decisions. She thought, "I may have created these ideas, but I truly believe them, and that's the way I am. I don't think I can change my unconscious thoughts, but maybe I can stop waiting for my relationships to get better and do something different. I could start by telling my boss what bothers me about my job and see if we can make any changes. I could tell my husband how unhappy I am."

Getting unstuck by using memories

Another way to do early memory work is to think about how many times you have heard yourself or someone else say, "I don't understand where this behavior comes from." Going back into your memories to gather information can help you breakthrough reoccurring and long-standing problems.

To do this, start by thinking of a problem. Remembering a recent time you were struggling with the problem can help you focus. Next, identify the type of relationship where the problem is occurring: work

I	Others	Life	Therefore
☑ I'm stupid. ☑ <u>I should know better.</u> ☑ I'm careful. ☑ I should take more time with things. ☑ I'm sneaky. ☑ <u>I take my time with things.</u> ☑ I put things off until it's too late. ☑ I have bad karma. ☑ I'm willing to wait, but I miss out. ☑ I want to be safe. ☑ I get embarrassed. ☑ I'm victimized.	☑ Others make fun of me. ☑ Others don't believe me. ☑ Others are in power and have control over me. ☑ Others give me a hard time. ☑ Others think they are right and don't listen to me. ☑ <u>Others stop me from having what's mine.</u> ☑ Others wreck things for me. ☑ Others are honest and better people than me. ☑ Others should know and do the right thing.	☑ Life is full of disappointments. ☑ Life is not fair. ☑ Life is hard. ☑ Life is serious. ☑ Life gives you something, then takes it away. ☑ <u>Life is a place where you don't get what you're entitled to.</u> ☑ Life is a place where things slip away when I don't pay attention.	☑ I should keep my mouth shut. ☑ I should be more careful. ☑ I shouldn't count on others to be fair. ☑ I agonize. ☑ I delay gratification. ☑ <u>I wait.</u> ☑ I seize opportunities. ☑ I keep to myself and nurse my anger, and I don't say how I feel. ☑ I have to guard against being a fool.

(or school), children, intimate relationships, self-esteem (relationship with self), spirituality (relationship to God/the universe), friendships, extended family, or community. Now, let a memory present itself that concerns your earliest experience of that kind of relationship. For example, if you chose work, think about your first work experience and see what memory comes to your mind. If you're struggling with children, remember one time in your childhood that you were having a problem with your parents. If it's about a friendship, what is your earliest memory about friendship? If it concerns an intimate relationship, what is your memory of your first boyfriend, girlfriend, or sexual experience? Write out the memory, including how old you were at the time, how you felt, and what you think your inner child decided. Make sure your decision sounds age appropriate: Would a five year old say it this way? An eleven year old?

Your memories hold a special gem that you can use to help you work on your current issue. After writing out the memory, underline the most vivid part. If your memory was a movie, you would enlarge that frame into a poster, capturing what it's about. Then write a sentence, beginning with the vivid part, add your feelings and end the sentence with your inner child's decision. It's easier than you think.

Harry's memory

"I was in high school and volunteered to build a booth for our club for a school fair. I designed the booth and then bought all the materials to make it. I worked on it entirely by myself. I designed and built the booth so it could be taken apart and reassembled. I couldn't be on hand the day of the fair to help put the booth together because I had to play in a basketball game, so I provided a set of instructions to assemble the booth. When I arrived at school after the basketball game, the booth was up but it looked awful. The students who had put it together did the best they could, but they were angry at me because they couldn't follow my instructions. I felt unappreciated, discouraged, and ashamed because I had to work the booth in the state it was in. I was 16 years old, and my 16-year-old decided, 'I can't let anybody help me—I have to do it all myself.'"

(**Harry's sentence:** "They were angry at me because they couldn't follow my instructions, and I felt unappreciated, discouraged, and ashamed—I have to do everything myself.")

Shane's memory

"I was doing my math homework and I asked my dad for help. Instead of guiding me through, he forced me to answer the problem myself. He didn't believe me when I said I didn't understand. I felt ashamed and criticized because Dad thought I knew it all along and that I was wasting his time. I was about 10 and my 10-year-old inner child decided not to ask for help anymore."

(**Shane's sentence:** He didn't believe that I didn't understand and I felt ashamed and criticized and decided not to ask for help anymore.)

Blythe's memory

"I was in junior high and best friends with Keesha, who was in string class, I was in wind instruments. She made friends with some girls in her section and I felt second-rate. But on Halloween, Keesha and I were invited to a party. We decided to go as twin clowns. I can see us getting on the public bus on our way to the party, dressed alike in big rubber feet, red noses, and wigs, with our faces painted white. We had on our fathers' pants, big shirts, neckties. The feeling of the memory is joyful. I was 13, and my 13-year-old inner child decided, 'I love being included and not treated as second rate.'"

(**Blythe's sentence:** We were getting on the bus and I felt joyful and decided, "I love being included and not treated as second rate.")

Dom's memory

"Peppi the parakeet was loose in my bedroom, so I chased him around trying to trap him under a cardboard box. When I finally slammed the box over him against the floor, it came down on his neck. I killed him. I felt horrified. I was five and my five-year-old inner child decided, "Oh, no, what have I done? I'm in trouble now."

(**Dom's sentence:** The box came down on his neck and I felt horrified and decided, "Oh, no, what have I done? I'm in trouble now.")

Putting it all together

By now you have thought of a current issue, written out your memory, and constructed a sentence like the four people in the examples above. As we put the information together for each of them, you may begin to see how your memory can help you make sense out of why you have been stuck. You will see what the deeper issues are that you need to address in order to move forward in the present.

Take Harry, who couldn't seem to find or hold a job. It was not because he lacked skills. Nor was it that he wasn't regularly looking for work—something else was holding him back. When he looked at the sentence he constructed, he said, "Working on this memory opened a door to a house I didn't know I lived in. I've been carrying so much shame around with me that I've been afraid to work. I think I figured out how to look like I was busy, while I was busy protecting myself from feeling more shame. I was also angry because I thought I had to do everything myself.

"Before learning about early memories, I thought my problems were caused by who I was—someone who couldn't count on others. Now I see that what I decided as a child led me to create the problems. Without realizing it, I created situations where no one could understand what I was doing so they couldn't help me. Then I ended up having to do everything myself, making me feel very angry. Maybe that's why I quit so many jobs or why employers let me go. Fortunately, my current job is set up so I can count on others to build what I design. They understand my needs and instructions and never let me down, which is probably why I am having so much fun and love working for this company."

Shane's current problem was dealing with his teenage daughter who was getting bad grades in school. The more time he spent trying to help her, the worse she did. She complained that she didn't understand her school work and Shane took her literally. He spent hours being available and helpful. He couldn't understand why his daughter didn't turn in the assignments they worked on together or why she was willing to let her grades drop.

When Shane looked at his memory he saw that he had decided to take his daughter seriously so she didn't have to feel the pain he did as a child when his father treated him like he was faking. Shane wanted his daughter to know that he would always be there for her and that she could ask for help anytime. What he realized, after working with his memory, was that his daughter already knew all that. He was a different father from his dad and his daughter had another agenda.

As he observed his daughter, Shane noticed that she never hesitated to do what needed to be done with activities that were important to her. She was happy to get Cs and even Ds in classes she thought weren't going to help her in her future. No amount of threatening, helping, or discussing was going to change her mind. Shane had to let his daughter be a separate person, even though it was difficult for him to stop jumping in to help.

When Blythe started her memory work, the issue she chose to focus on involved her friend Stephanie, who had invited someone else to help her plan an event for their charitable organization, passing Blythe by. At first she was confused by the vivid part of her memory, "We were getting on the bus...". How was this information supposed to help her with the issue she was dealing with? Then Blythe realized that maybe the "bus" signified something else. Why was she remembering a bus when she usually rode the subway? How was a bus different? "I get it," she thought, "The bus symbolizes going somewhere special, as opposed to the other means of transportation, which are what I normally do."

"Well," she thought, "it is important for me to go somewhere, just like in junior high, when I wanted to be somebody special. But I'm not interested in going somewhere unless I'm with friends, and I hate it when they pass me by."

Blythe decided to share the memory and her awareness with Stephanie, who responded first by giving her a hug and then said, "Blythe, I asked Ingrid to help me because you have been so busy and doing so much. I thought it was time someone else took a turn at doing some of the hard work around here so we could give you a little break. I never meant to leave you out or imply you weren't good enough, and I'm sorry that your feelings are hurt. Don't you know how much we all respect and admire you in this organization?"

Dom used the memory work to learn more about how he fit in. He often saw himself as a loner. When he wrote out his sentence, he was puzzled because he couldn't imagine how a dead parakeet's head sticking out from under a box could help him understand any part of his current situation. "I don't even have a parakeet," he said. What Dom needed to do was translate some of his information. You may find that you have to do the same thing to be able to understand what you've uncovered.

The dead parakeet, like the bus in Blythe's memory, represents something else—it's a metaphor for Dom. Looking at the first part of the sentence, Dom realized that the dead parakeet symbolized a mistake. Dom then thought about all the ways he stayed quiet and kept to the sidelines. If he made a mistake, no one would notice and he wouldn't get in trouble. No wonder he thought he didn't fit in. It wasn't that he was quiet or shy—he stayed withdrawn as a safety net to stay out of trouble. Dom also noticed that the only person he was in trouble with when the parakeet died was himself. He was punishing himself and putting himself in a jail of his own for accidentally killing the parakeet. Without realizing, the adult Dom still feared the imagined catastrophes his inner 5 year old conjured up. Dom felt sad that he had killed his parakeet, but he realized that mistakes he made while becoming involved as an adult in activities and relationships wouldn't cause irreversible harm.

Additional uses of early memories

Patricia complained about her husband incessantly, but was sure that if she waited long enough, he would change into the person she could love. She threatened divorce on more than one occasion and even moved out for a short time, thinking a separation would shock Jake into getting his act together. The situation continued to slide downhill until Patricia did some early memory work. To begin, she focused on a recent situation with Jake and then thought of an early memory.

Patricia's memory

"I was at an amusement park for the first time and saw the merry-go-round. I wanted to ride it so badly, but I was afraid and said so. Dave, my 19-year-old cousin, leaned over when he heard me say I was afraid, and whispered in my ear, 'How about if we go on the merry-go-round together?' I smiled, taking his hand. We both climbed onto the ride. As the ride started, he stood at my side with his arm around me. I noticed the brass rings and asked what they were for. He said I could reach out and grab one. Again, I said I was afraid; I thought I might fall. He said, 'I'll hold you.' 'But what if I still fall?' I asked, and he said, 'Then I'll fall with you.' I felt very loved. I decided I liked being with my cousin and that he was nice."

After looking at the memory she had written, Patricia thought, "No wonder I'm not happy in my marriage. I'm looking for a completely different person. I want someone like my cousin, and my husband is nothing like that. I don't like him the way he is. I'm asking him to change who he is, not what he does, and that's not fair. He can't do that, so I really need to look at why I'm still living with him. I wanted someone who would hold me up and fall with me if I made a mistake, like the little girl in my memory. In our marriage, I'm holding Jake up. I spoil him because I want to be spoiled, and I think if I do for him what I'd like him to do for me, he'll get the picture. Now I realize he'll never get the picture."

There are still more treasures Patricia had yet to uncover, so she used three new tools that made her memory a great help to her. The first tool was to talk to her five-year-old inner child and find out what she needed. The second was to do a reality check. Finally, she used a "magic wand" to rewrite her memory the way she wanted it to be.

Tool 1: Ask your inner child what he or she needs

The easiest way to do this is to picture a place where you could sit next to your inner child and have a chat. You might sit on a couch, a log, or a swing. In your mind, pretend your inner child is with you and is telling you what he or she needs. Then recall a child you know who is currently the age your inner child was in the memory. This will help you be sensitive to your inner child's needs. If your inner child is birth to three years old, try rocking or cuddling; three to six, go to the park or bake cookies; six to 10, a movie and popcorn; for a preadolescent inner child, write in your diary; and for a full-blown teenager, go out for pizza, CDs, or clothes.

Patricia pictured sitting on the bench at the amusement park with her arm around her inner five year old, who sat on her lap. When she asked her little child what she needed, little Patricia said, "I want my cousin Dave to be with me. He takes good care of me and will keep me safe." Patricia told her inner child, "Dave isn't here, but I'll keep you safe. Let's start by telling Jake how unhappy you are."

Tool 2: Do a reality check

Whenever Patricia felt unhappy about her marriage with Jake, she reverted back to her five-year-old inner child. Even though Jake saw a grown woman, what he didn't realize is that he was actually relating to five-year-old Patricia. What he saw was a mopey, pouty, sullen person, which is the way Patricia dealt with problems when she was five. With this tool, Patricia once again pictured someone she knew who was five years old so that she could get a clear idea of how a child that age looks and acts. Thinking about the five year old down the block brought a smile to Patricia's face, as she realized the emotional age of the person inside her, trying to cope in her marriage. No wonder Jake wasn't responding well to her efforts at communication. This information encouraged Patricia, by helping her to be less hard on herself. She gave herself time to cool down when she was upset, using her adult words to communicate with Jake later.

Tool 3: Use a "wand" to rescript your memory

Pretending to have a magic wand is an easy way to find out how you solve problems or how you would like life to be. When Patricia "waved" her wand over her memory, Dave was on all the rides with her. Her magic wand solution showed Patricia that she wanted someone in her life who acted like Dave all the time. Was she living in denial thinking Jake could be like Dave? Was Jake ever like Dave?

After using these three tools, Patricia had a lot to think about and had many questions. Was she in the right marriage? Did she invite unhealthy responses from Jake because she acted like a five-year-old girl when she felt unloved? Would it be possible for them to heal their relationship if she shared her memory and decisions with Jake?

The last question scared her, because she didn't want Jake to get mad and yell or drive off and stay away for hours. "When he acts that way, emotionally, I'm only five years old, and I'm not old enough to stay home alone. Maybe I could at least tell Jake that." Using the three tools for changing early memories, Patricia had some avenues to pursue to get out of the impasse, and she felt better.

Discovering and healing past issues

Patricia isn't the only one who can act like a five year old when she's upset. You may have found yourself or others acting in a way that seems inappropriate or out of proportion. What was happening at that time is that something in the situation—a word, a sound, a smell, a phrase, an action—triggered some unfinished business from your childhood. Unconsciously, you or another person acted like a scared little child inside. Once you start down that trail, it's almost impossible to grow up quickly enough in that moment to become rational. The more you've held inside, the greater the reaction. This can include full-blown panic attacks and nightmares.

When we do early memory work, we ask you to state your feelings and decisions along with the memory. Feelings are energy, and if feelings are repressed over a long period of time, they tend to come out in extreme ways. The same can be true when you don't examine your childhood decisions. Take a look at the cone on the right. Imagine putting a feeling or a thought in its original form in the pointed end of the cone. As the feeling or thought is denied, pushed down, or disrespected, it  builds and grows, even though it's contained. By the time the feeling or thought reaches the outer limits of the cone, it is hugely distorted. When an event cracks the cone, the distortion emerges.

There are many names for these distortions: bad trips, nervous breakdowns, anxiety attacks, chemical imbalances, post-traumatic stress syndrome, among others. Rather than only treating the problem with drugs, it is important to go back to the original thought or feeling and start the healing process. You can do this by using your memories.

Some of the events that especially invite a person to keep thoughts and feelings repressed are early childhood emotional abuse, physical or sexual abuse, and overcontrolling, permissive, addicted, or neglectful parents. If you have lived through any of these situations, you may be aware first hand of how much shame and pain a person can carry. As a child, you may have decided you were bad or that bad situations were your fault. You may have disregarded events because they were too painful or frightening. Or if they didn't fit with the reality you had already formed, you may have hidden the feelings that went with them, as well as the decisions you made. You may not remember, as an adult, why you think or feel the way you do. As a child, perhaps you found a way to mentally and emotionally escape, because of your suffering. Some of our clients visualized escaping through a crack in the ceiling. Others imagined leaving their bodies and going somewhere safe. One young man who had been repeatedly beaten as a child imagined going to the end of his block. He didn't dare go any farther even in his fantasy because he said, "I wasn't allowed to cross the street unless an adult was with me."

If you start having uncomfortable memories, feelings or thoughts, we hope you will let them out using early memory work and not try to control and hide them from yourself any longer.

Jasmine's story

Jasmine was visiting with friends on a weekend ski trip. She and eight other skiers were sitting around the table having a potluck dinner. Suddenly, Jasmine started to feel queasy and wasn't sure why. Maybe it was the pot of beans cooking on the stove, she wasn't sure. Jasmine realized she often got a stomach ache if she thought about or saw a pot of beans. When she was home, she tried to solve the problem by never buying or eating beans. But there were times, like now, that it was out of her control. Jasmine didn't want to make a scene, so she tried to ignore the feeling.

A few minutes later, Brant, one of the members of the group said, "Hey, Jas, aren't you going to thank me for carrying your skis today?" Not feeling well, Jasmine ignored the comment and said nothing, but her friend repeated, "Jas, you owe me a big thank you. Don't keep me waiting." Even though he was smiling when he told Jasmine what to do, she felt her stomach tighten and thought she might throw up. Struggling to maintain control, she said nothing. Getting no response, Brant stood up and started walking towards Jasmine, looking as though he might touch her. Jasmine stood up and screamed, "Get away from me. I can't take it. Leave me alone. I've had enough." The others sat in shocked silence, trying to figure out what had just happened, as Jasmine ran sobbing to her car and drove away.

The next day, a friend of Jasmine's who had been at the dinner, called to find out how she was doing. Jasmine said, "I'm so humiliated and embarrassed. Can you guys ever forgive me?" Her friend said no one was angry, just confused. Jasmine replied, "This is hard for me to say, but I think I know what happened because I've been working with my memories. When I got home, I did some writing in my journal, and I think I put it together. Are you sure you want to hear?" "Of course I do," her friend replied.

"I think I may have been molested when I was a little girl. I had a flashback last night and I pictured a house that was down the lane from our home. I remembered going inside to see their new kittens. I must have been about four years old. The man who lived there did something bad to hurt me. I was crying and trying to leave. He held up one of the kittens over the pot of beans on his stove and said, 'If you tell anyone what just happened, I'll kill your whole family and I'll cut up this kitten and put it in the beans.' I think the combination of seeing the pot of beans last night and Brant telling me I had to thank him and then coming towards me triggered something. My emotions felt like they were on a dimmer switch. When I first saw the beans my feelings were pretty dim and by the time Brant stood up and started walking towards me, I was at full intensity. I hope I didn't scare anyone, but I think it was good for me to yell stop, because I couldn't do that when I was a kid."

Jasmine was healing past issues. The work had rough edges, but holding in the feelings had been making Jasmine sick.

How overcompensations begin

When you were born, you were good enough just the way you were. In the course of growing up, you made a faulty decision that you weren't good enough. In order to be good enough, you would have to be a certain way or achieve a certain status or goal. You started overcompensating to prove your worth. The more you overcompensated, the farther you got from your true self and the more stress you created in your life. Look at the diagram below:

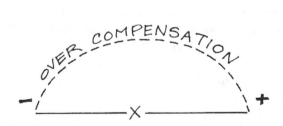

The line stands for your life, the X is you at birth, the minus is your faulty perception of yourself not being good enough. The plus is where you think you need to go to prove yourself. The dotted line that connects the minus with the plus stands for overcompensation.

As a child, Jasmine had decided she was at fault when her neighbor molested her, and that decision changed her. Before the molestation, she was a happy-go-lucky little girl. After the incident, she decided that she was bad. Without realizing any positive solutions, she compensated by feeling worthless.

Jasmine's self-esteem had been badly damaged. Instead of being her cheerful self, she became quiet and refused to go anywhere alone. She spent hours in her room with her coloring books. Later in life, she continued her art, which she enjoyed, but she always felt a part of her had disappeared. She knew that for her art was an escape, a way to prove to the world that she was worthwhile. Although she received many accolades for her watercolors, inside she never believed she was good enough.

When the incident at the potluck occurred, she was dating a policeman whom she didn't like very much. After she worked with her memories, she became aware that she might be going out with him because she thought he could keep her safe. The four year old within still needed protection. Jasmine was able to break off the relationship when she realized that she was capable of taking care of herself. Her independence was growing, and she felt like her old self was returning.

(!) Hint   Tips to keep memory work safe

1. Add a support group or therapist to your do-it-yourself therapy to get past the difficult parts.

2. Picture a container into which you can put your feelings, memories, or thoughts when you don't want to work on them anymore. Make a deal with yourself that you will only open the container when you are ready to work. Some people picture a box with a lock, others an urn, others a jar with a lid.

3. Create safe ways to express anger. You can pound nails into a board, break old dishes against a wall, pound holes in newspaper held between two people, punch a pillow. You can get in your car, roll up the windows and scream as loud as you like and not be heard (of course, don't drive until you're calm).

4. When you're feeling especially stressed, use a journal to write until you can't write anymore. If you are too agitated to write, make circles with your pen or use the broad side of peeled crayons or pastels to scribble until you tire.

5. Ask your friends to be available either in person or on the phone for a hug or to listen without trying to fix anything for you.

Jasmine was working on giving up "either/or" thinking. In the past, she had believed that either she was a successful artist or that she was a nobody, unworthy of love. As she worked more with her memories, she began to see that she had choices. Breaking up with her boyfriend was one of them; sharing her memory work with her friend was another. Eventually, Jasmine was convinced that she didn't have to prove anything. She wasn't a bad person who had no worth—her early decisions had been triggered by someone else hurting her.

If you think back, you can probably pinpoint the time when your self-esteem was damaged. It's not what happened to you, but what you decided about the event that started you down a trail of overcompensation. Close your eyes and let a memory come to mind. Look at the memory, the feelings, and the decisions with adult eyes. See if you can discover how you have overcompensated to prove your worth. It is human nature to believe that you have to behave in a certain way so that no one will find out how you really are, but we hope that after reading our book, you will know that it's fine the way you are, and that many of your thoughts, feelings, and behaviors are ways of overcompensating. Doing early memory work can help bring you back to who you really are. Your early memories tell a story about your personal experience, but your history is one you created based on the decisions you made. With understanding and optimism you can rewrite your history and be yourself.

 ## Creating changes in your world

After reading this chapter, you've learned that your memories are thumbnail sketches that tell you how you think, feel, and what you decided. Memories are reflections of your inner child and what that child needs to heal. Your memories hold rich treasures that can help you reclaim your true self and your self-esteem. Use the activities that have already been introduced in the chapter along with the additional suggestions in this section to help you make changes in your world.

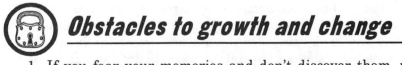 ## Obstacles to growth and change

1. If you fear your memories and don't discover them, you'll miss out on learning more about the person you are.
2. If you are judgmental and critical with your inner child, you might discourage yourself before you start.

3. If you try to stifle your thoughts and feelings with drugs or avoidance, you'll miss out on the solutions within.

4. If you say that you don't remember anything and won't try, you will not be able to use the information in this chapter.

5. If you hide from others, and don't share what you're learning from your early memories, you won't have the additional perspective of looking at your private logic through others' separate realities.

6. If you get the same memory or same few memories when you think about your childhood, and think the work is wasted because you're not remembering anything new, you'll miss out on all the riches in the memory that is in front of you.

Easy steps for change

☑ Write out as many of your early memories as you can to use to help you in your work.

☑ Look at the memories you wrote down and see how old you were. That is the age of the "inner consultant" who has information for you or who needs healing. Think of ways to talk to that child within.

☑ Write out your earliest memory. It is the clearest statement of who you are. Ask for help to brainstorm the "I," "Other," "Life," and "Therefore" statements so you can learn more about your private logic.

☑ Think about a situation that is troubling you and use one of your early memories to find inspiration to move forward.

☑ If you can't think of any memories, make some up. They'll still work to help you uncover your separate reality.

☑ When all else fails, use your photo albums to help you trigger your childhood memories.

 ## Activities

1. Pretend you have a magic wand. Go back into your childhood with the wand and change the events you would like to be different, using your imagination. Write about what the events are, how you would change them, and how your life would be different once you have made the changes.

2. Draw one of your early memories. You don't have to be artistic to do this. You can use circles, squares, or stick figures. If you have people in the memory, put a dialogue bubbles over their heads and give them something to say. Give the picture a title. Write about what the picture tells you about your private logic.

3. Picture your inner child and give that child a voice. Write down whatever the child is telling you and see how you can use the information to help you solve a current life situation.

4. Keep a memory journal. You will be amazed to see how your memories evolve as you change. Notice even the slightest variation and use it to help you track your progress. One woman remembered being on a patio riding her tricycle in circles. Later, after working on her therapy, she remembered being on her patio riding her tricycle and noticing a door on the patio. Later still she pictured herself pushing the bike to the patio walls and looking over the top. Each memory represented the progress she was making.

5. Notice when one of your memories has a new feeling associated with it. As you work on your therapy, you'll see that your work gives you a more positive outlook. If you have a memory with a new feeling associated with it, write about what has changed in your life.

6. Ask others to tell you what they see in your memories, as it is often difficult to be objective. You remember what fits with your private logic, so you need other people's perspectives to help you see what you might be missing. If what they see doesn't fit for you, don't use it.

 **Week 6**

Learn Why You Do What You Do

Changing the way that you think about behavior will be some of the most powerful therapy you will ever do. This week you will have an opportunity to change your thinking about a question frequently asked but rarely understood: "Why do people do what they do?" If you subscribe to today's conventional wisdom, you're probably looking for what causes people to behave the way they do. You search for a cause outside the person, something out of his or her control. You may think the cause is a traumatic event or something wrong in the environment or a situation. You might say something like: "He had a bad childhood." "She's having trouble in her marriage." "His brother just died."

Perhaps you search for a cause inside the person, a defect or character flaw that "explains" the behavior and tack on a label to complete the scenario, like: he or she is a slacker, ignoramus, fool, witch, lazy bum, jerk, control freak, crazy, nympho, meanie—the list goes on and on.

Or maybe you look for a disease and come up with a diagnosis: "She is an alcoholic." "He has a learning disability." "He has attention deficit disorder." "She is suffering from a depression."

Over the last three decades the search for causes for people's behavior has led to a lack of personal responsibility, resulting in a lot of unhappy, victimized people. People do not recognize their own role in difficulties if they look for something or someone else to blame. Deciding that inappropriate behavior is caused by some event, illness, circumstance, genetic feature, personality flaw, or another person, you are rendered powerless.

All behavior has a purpose

Instead of labeling behavior as a symptom of a character defect, or as a reaction to an event, we see behavior as having a purpose—a goal. Humans have the same primary goals: To belong and to be significant. As a member of the human race, you want to belong and have a unique identity within your group. That group could be your family or any other community you take part in (your school, neighborhood, workplace, or a team). When you feel encouraged and have that "I belong, can-do attitude," your behavior is a way you seek belonging and significance. You do it in useful ways by connecting, cooperating with others, contributing, and acting with consideration and compassion.

When you are discouraged, you can also search for belonging and significance in useless ways. This would mean that you don't feel connected to others, don't have faith in your ability to solve tasks, are more involved in competing than cooperating, and focus on what you will get instead of on what contribution you can make.

The four goals all people have

Instead of asking *why* people do what they do, we suggest that you ask *what* the purpose of their behavior is. We have been profoundly influenced by Rudolf Dreikurs and Vicki Soltz's book, *Children: The Challenge*. This book laid out for the first time the mistaken goals of behavior. We have expanded this information by showing that all people (including you) look for belonging and significance by seeking recognition, power, justice, and skills. All your behavior is an unconscious attempt to accomplish one or more of these goals in either a useful, encouraged way or a useless, discouraged way.

The first goal, **recognition**, is a sense of acknowledgment and appreciation. You need to know that you are unique and special.

The second goal of **power** is about finding a sense of control in your world. This might be the freedom to make choices and decisions, or the ability to anticipate or plan how the day or the week will go. Or, power can be the knowledge that ultimately you can do what you want.

Justice is the third goal. You've often heard that life isn't fair. Yet you strive to ensure that there is fairness in your life and in the world around you. You want the world to be a place where people care about

Ways we pursue the four goals		
The Goal	Useful pursuits, leading to encouragement	Useless pursuits, leading to discouragement
Recognition	☑ Volunteer or ask for time.	☑ Demand incessant attention.
Power	☑ Ask for what you want.	☑ Engage in power struggles.
Justice	☑ Make amends for your mistakes.	☑ Get even, seeking revenge.
Skills	☑ Take small steps to accomplish hard tasks.	☑ Give up before you start.

you, where it's okay to be you, and where you won't be abused because of who you are.

The fourth goal, **skills**, is knowing you can handle what happens in life, whether it's daily tasks, getting along with people, special projects, or sudden challenges. You want to be able to learn, know that you can do well, and that you can be successful.

When you meet your goals in useful ways, you are proactive. You think first about the needs of the situation and your responses are encouraging. When you behave in useless ways, you are reactive, responding to your feelings, not considering how your behavior impacts yourself and others.

Here are a few examples of people whose reactive behaviors take them into the land of discouragement. First is Simon, who waits over a half hour for his brother to show up and feels annoyed once again. Yet, he makes excuses for him, because he isn't "responsible" like Simon. When Mindy's boss scolds her in front of a customer, she swallows her anger, rationalizing that his behavior stems from a miserable marriage, and that it's her fault because she made a mistake. Grace feels disappointed in herself decides she is a weak person with no restraint when she eats the leftover Halloween candy in her son's bedroom. Finally, Whitney is in despair, believing her husband is addicted to sex, which would explain why he has affairs and isn't able to change.

By following our three-step plan, Simon, Mindy, Grace, and Whitney you can learn to break the "code" of behavior and find how underlying goals work in their life—and so can you.

Breaking the code of behavior

People's actions are like coded statements. You can be a "codebreaker" by focusing on the purpose of a behavior, instead of on the behavior itself. Instead of defining misbehavior as a character defect or an emotional illness, think of it as a form of discouragement. You can identify which goal is operating in the behavior, whether it is recognition, power, justice, or skills. Then you can attend to the mistaken thinking and discover options to help you and others feel more encouraged. Our three steps will help you will need to recognize your feelings in order to identify their goal. Then, notice what you did when you had the feeling and what the result was. Finally, choose a new response that is both proactive and encouraging, instead of reactive and discouraging.

Step 1: Recognize your feelings to identify the goal

Think of a time when you felt irritated, annoyed, worried, angry, frustrated, hurt, disgusted, disappointed, hopeless, helpless, or despair in response to some behavior. These feelings are a signal that you and/or someone you are relating to has slipped into the land of discouragement. Your feelings are much like the dashboard lights in your car. When your feelings switch on, they indicate that something has just happened that you need to deal with it to avoid bigger problems. Much like your dash lights, your feelings can help you identify what the problem is so you can make an informed decision about what to do.

Different feelings give you different information about what is going on below the surface. Remember, the behavior is what you see on the outside and the goal of behavior is what is underneath. The chart on page 138 shows which feelings indicate which goal and clarify the mistaken thinking of each of the goals.

Notice the mistaken beliefs that go with each kind of discouragement. If you are thinking in a discouraged way, your resulting behavior will be what we call mischief. As you read the following stories, you will see how people used mischief. Usually, if one person uses mischief and another person responds without knowing the goals of behavior, the amount of mischief multiplies exponentially. Individual mischief becomes relationship mischief, whether the relationship is with another person or with yourself.

Midori's story

Midori often took her young son to the neighborhood playground in the afternoons, where she met with a group of other mothers. While she enjoyed having adult company, she noticed that one of the women complained nonstop about her husband's thoughtlessness. Midori found herself feeling irritated and began to sit as far from her as possible on the benches. This behavior prompted "Mrs. Whiner" to wait a few minutes and try again to get Midori's attention with a new story. Once she read about the purpose of behavior, Midori recognized that "Mrs. Whiner," whose name was really Amanda, was seeking **recognition** in the group, though she was going about it in an annoying way. Midori realized, "Maybe I'm doing mischief by being rude and avoiding her."

Julie's story

Julie was looking for a job and reading *Do-It-Yourself Therapy* to direct her. When she read the "help wanted" section in the newspaper, she noticed that whenever an item caught her eye, she immediately thought of all the reasons the job wouldn't work for her. In this way, she stopped herself from following up on every job opportunity. Feeling **angry** and frustrated, she thought, "But I really want a different job. Why do I dismiss everything before I even get started? I have to stop behaving this way right now."

When she looked at the "Feelings/Goals/Thinking Chart" on page 138, Julie noticed that anger was one of the feelings that accompanies a need for power. She wondered who she could possibly have issues with. It finally occurred to her that she was in a power struggle with herself, trying to do something that didn't fit for her. As a child everything seemed to come easy for her brother, but she had to struggle to achieve what she wanted. Her inner child was telling her, "You'll never find a job without a struggle," and "You'll never be as successful as your brother." How was she ever going to get the little child out of the land of discouragement when that child was kicking and screaming?

Gina's story

When their mother died, Gina and her brother Travis inherited her modest estate. Gina was thrilled. She had waited a long time to be able to afford some things, and took great pleasure in purchasing them immediately. Travis, on the other hand, set to work calculating how he could

Feelings/goals/thinking chart	
If you feel	**There is probably an underlying issue involving:**
Worried **Anxious** **Irritated** **Annoyed**	Issues with recognition, appreciation, identity, and/or specialness. *"Are people watching me? Do they know who I am? Will they do things for me that I could do for myself, to prove their love? Am I the most special? Am I appreciated?"*
Angry **Defeated** **Frustrated** **Challenged**	Issues with power or control. *"No one can tell me what to do. I am the boss of me. No one can boss me around. I can do what I want."*
Hurt **Disgusted** **Disappointed** **Upset or sad**	Issues with justice, fairness, or acceptance. *"This isn't fair. Someone hurt me, so I'll even the score. Nobody cares about me, so I don't care about them. There is no justice, so I don't have to follow the rules either."*
Hopeless **Helpless** **Despair**	Issues with skills, ability, perfection, or competence. *"No matter what I do, I cannot do it good enough, so what's the point of trying? I won't try because it won't be perfect and I don't want to be embarrassed. Everyone else is better than me, so why bother?"*

make his part of the estate go as far as possible to benefit his family, investing in his children's college funds and his retirement plan. Every time Gina talked to Travis, he seemed distant and uninterested in what she had to say. He found ways to put her down and insinuate that she was a spoiled, irresponsible brat. Her feelings were hurt. As she learned more about using her feelings as a guide to uncover the goals of behavior, Gina guessed that under her hurt feelings was a **justice** issue.

Gavin's story

Gavin's wife June was in chronic pain. She had a headache or a stomach ache most of the time. She was seeing less and less of her friends and opting out of many of the activities she enjoyed. Gavin thought she must be clinically depressed. A cycling enthusiast who had been interested in health most of his life, Gavin was convinced that June would feel better if she stopped eating high-fat, low-fiber foods and started exercising. He cooked special meals to show her how delicious healthy eating could be, stocked the kitchen with nutritious food, and invited her to go bike riding with him. June complained that it was too overwhelming to change her eating habits and that she was too tired and in too much pain to ride bikes.

When Gavin learned about the purpose of behavior and mischief, he realized June might not have a chronic disease but rather issues about **skills**. This helped him rethink his interactions with June.

You can use these stories or a personal situation to practice your new skills in code breaking. First, notice the feelings each person had. Then look at the chart above and match the feelings with the appropriate goal and mistaken thinking. What was the goal of the problem behavior in your situation? You probably noticed that Amanda's goal was recognition, Julie's power, Gina's justice, and June's skills. Think about how each of their reactions kept everyone discouraged.

Rebecca's story

At this point, it is tempting to assume that certain behaviors indicate certain goals. But it's not the behavior that is the clue as to what the goal is—it's your feelings that indicate the goal of the behavior. See how lateness can cause issues.

Rebecca's boyfriend is always late. His discouragement might be aimed at achieving recognition and attention by being a character who can never be on time. Rebecca knows his behavior is mischievous when she feels irritated. He might manage to be punctual for the next time or two, but then reverts right back to his old ways.

But if she feels angry or defeated as she checks your watch, and demands that he stop dragging his feet, his goal is power. On the other hand, if she feels hurt or disgusted as she cools your heels while the minutes tick by, then stomps into the bathroom hissing, "Do you realize what an inconsiderate jerk you are?!" only to be treated to a wordless ride to the party and a cold shoulder for the evening, what she has are justice and fairness issues.

Step 2: What was the result of your reaction?

Now that you have learned how to recognize your feelings and identify their goals, work on noticing what you did when you had those feelings. Ask yourself what happened as a result of your reactive behavior. When relating to a discouraged person who is using mischief (including yourself), chances are good that any automatic response on anyone's part will lead to more mischief.

Go back to the stories once again and see how each person reacted to mischief and then notice what happened. You may have noticed that Midori avoided Amanda, who stopped momentarily and then renewed her efforts with a different complaint. Julie forced herself to look for a job, and then used passive power, allowing her never to get hired. Gina withheld her hurt feelings from her brother while attacking him in her mind, while her brother handled his feelings of disgust and jealousy with sarcasm, instead of honesty. And when Gavin became overly helpful, June was more passive and withdrawn. On the chart on page 141, you can see the typical mischief that occurs when you react to discouraged behavior. The reactive responses in the first column are just as discouraged as those in the second.

Mischief plus mischief equals more mischief. If what you are doing doesn't improve a situation and you and others feel even more discouraged, it's time to move on to Step 3 to find a more encouraging response.

Step 3: Respond proactively

The chart on page 141 shows you what typical mischief responses are. Then, the chart on pages 142-143 summarizes what your options are for helping yourself and others meet relationship needs in useful ways. People don't behave in these ways without thought and practice, but when you adopt these behaviors, you'll find that you feel better. We find that a shortcut for successfully using Step 3 is to look in column three. Picture a person who is misbehaving asking for what is in the third column. When you can respond accordingly, most mischief disappears. After looking at the chart, notice how the people in the stories used the information to improve their situations. (Roslyn Duffy, co-author of many of the *Positive Discipline* books, created these simple messages to use to help the parents of preschoolers be more encouraging.)

Midori breaks the code

Midori realized that Amanda's goal was to find recognition. So, the next time she headed for the park, Midori went with a plan to notice and involve Amanda before she started her whiny behavior. As Midori entered the park she smiled and motioned for Amanda to sit beside her. Amanda seemed pleased but surprised. After telling Amanda how nice it was to see her, she looked at her watch and said, "I have five minutes to chat, and then I promised I'd push Tyler on the swings. We made a deal, and I really like to keep my promises. Don't you? Could you help me out and remind me when it's 3:15?" Amanda responded with an enthusiastic, "I'd be happy to." She

Mischief Responses

If your reactive response includes any of the following, you are practicing mischief.	If others' responses include any of the following, they are practicing mischief.	The purpose of such behavior is probably to attain:
Giving energy and attention to another person or situation. Coaxing. Fixing or trying to fix a problem. Doing something for others they could do for themselves. Bailing out or rescuing. Reminding or nagging others. Doing extra work. Stopping what you're doing to focus on others. Trying to avoid others, thinking "This person occupies too much of my time." Pampering.	Temporarily changes behavior, but later resumes with the same or another annoying behavior. Performs or responds only when getting attention. Manipulates.	Recognition Acknowledgment Appreciation Specialness (Like Midori and Amanda)
Defending yourself, your ideas, or your actions. Fighting. Bossing. Overpowering. Defying. Thinking, "You can't get away with that," "I'll make you," or "I won't and you can't make me." Trying to be right. Controlling. Giving in.	Escalating or intensifying the behavior. Using passive power. Thinking, "I've won," after making the other person upset.	Power Control (Like Julie)
Intensifying. Getting even, retaliating, seeking revenge. Taking the behavior personally. Withdrawing. Withholding. Punishing. Judging. Being critical. Thinking, "How could you do this to me?"	Intensifying. Counterattacking, hurting back, getting even, retaliating, or seeking revenge. Acting mean. Back stabbing. Hurting strangers. Escalating the same behavior or choosing another weapon. Withdrawing. Withholding. Punishing. Judging. Being critical.	Justice Fairness (Like Trevor and Gina)
Helping too much. Taking over. Doing for. Giving up. Not expecting anything.	Retreating further. Being passive. Not improving. Not responding. Giving up completely. Withdrawing. Avoiding others.	Skills Competence Ability (Like Gavin and June)

☹☺ Turning discouragment into encouragment ☺

If someone is using mischief to pursue:	The unconscious mistaken belief behind the behavior is:	Picture the person saying:	To improve the relationship instead of feeding the discouragement, your options include:
Recognition **Acknowledgment** **Appreciation** **Specialness**	I know I belong and am special when people notice me or do things for me I could do for myself. I know I'm important when I can keep others busy with me or get special service. No one appreciates what I do. If you loved me, you would _____ (fill in the blank).	Notice me. Involve me.	Give attention on your own terms. Set up a special time to give the person or situation attention. Say how you feel and what you want. Tell the person he or she is special. Use nonverbal signals or smile. Say "Good try." Say "I love you." Separate yourself physically from him/her. Set your limits and follow through. Set up routines. Ignore the mischief. Avoid undue service or pampering.
Power **Control**	No one can tell me what to do or be the boss of me. People are trying to boss me around, but they can't make me do anything. I can do whatever I want. I count when I win. I'm important if you do what I tell you. I belong and am special when I get my way and you do what I want. I know best and I'm right.	Let me help. Give me choices.	Don't fight and don't give in; withdraw from the conflict. Admit you can't make the person do what you want. Ask for help and for the person's input. Give choices. Say how you feel and what you want. Say that you're angry. Take a break and talk later. Say "I'll be back." Cool off and work toward a solution later. Get out of "right and wrong" thinking and acknowledge differences. Agree to disagree. Ask, "Are you feeling overpowered? How?" Decide what you're going to do to satisfy yourself.

☺ Turning discouragment into encouragment ☺

If someone is using mischief to pursue:	The unconscious mistaken belief behind the behavior is:	Picture the person saying:	To improve the relationship instead of feeding the discouragement, your options include:
Justice Fairness	I belong by hurting others, as I feel hurt. I can't be liked or loved. It's not fair; there's no justice. People are mean to me. Nobody cares; people don't care about me so I don't care about them either. Someone can hurt me, so I'll even the score; I'll get even and make them pay.	Help me. I'm hurting.	Acknowledge the other's hurt feelings. Use reflective listening. Be a friend. Give a hug. Show you care. Apologize. Make amends. Avoid retaliating. Avoid feeling hurt yourself, try not to take the other's behavior personally. Say how you feel. Wait to problem solve until the friendship is repaired.
Skills Ability Competence	I can't belong because I'm not good enough. I want everyone to leave me alone because I can't do things properly. No matter what I do I'll eventually fail. I can't. Everyone else is better than me. I'll never do that. It's too late. I'm too old. I can't be perfect, so I won't try at all. I belong by convincing others not to expect anything of me. I am helpless and unable; it's no use trying.	Believe in me. Don't give up on me.	Take small steps. Find a way to get started. Don't give up on the person. Let the person know you have faith in him or her. Tell the person you know he or she will do things when ready. Stop all criticism. Encourage any positive attempt, no matter how small. Focus on assets. Don't pity. Offer chances for success. Teach skills/show how. Step back. Offer help if asked, "I'm here if you want help." Ask if the person would like to be shown. Make it safe to ask for help; say, "It's okay to make mistakes, they are opportunities to learn." Listen without giving advice. Do things with, not for, the person.

then proceeded to tell a story about her husband's latest rudeness, to which Midori interrupted and said, "Amanda, I'd love to hear more about you, but these marriage problems are getting me down. Do you mind if we talk about something else? Tell me where you found those cute shoes you're wearing." Without missing a beat, Amanda switched to the subject of her shoes while keeping one eye on her watch. At exactly 3:15 p.m., she said, "Time for Tyler. Thanks for listening. See you tomorrow." Midori felt much less discouraged and actually enjoyed listening to Amanda.

Julie breaks the code

As Julie looked at the goals of behavior, she wondered how she felt and what she wanted. She was so used to focusing on being different from her brother that she never took the time to be clear about her own goals. Julie decided to start writing in a journal to clarify how she was feeling. She started by asking herself if she really wanted to find a new job and answered, yes. Then she decided to be more specific and write down what she wanted in a job. She told herself, "I may not get everything I want, but at least I'll narrow my search and look for work

① Hint   Degrees of discouragement

You may think that someone who has a skills-based issue is more discouraged than a person who craves recognition, but we believe that none of the goals indicates any more discouragement than do the others. Discouragement can vary considerably in depth and intensity for all four relationship needs.

Imagine a scale of one to 10. If you were seeking recognition and attention and your level of discouragement was a two, you might be gossiping, tattling, talking too much, interrupting someone's conversations, or distracting someone with irrelevant behavior. But if you're seeking recognition and are discouraged with a level of 10, you may be robbing the liquor store or threatening suicide to get your name in the paper. As you noticed in the example about lateness, a behavior can start as one goal and end up as another. This often happens when you react to mischief with mischief—the situation only gets worse.

What begins as a need for recognition becomes a power struggle. Power struggles that go on and on often lead to revenge, and after a time, you may begin to feel hopeless and helpless and give up.

that meets my needs." Her list included a short commute, an active environment, variety, a flexible schedule, with little to no paper shuffling. Going through the want ads was a lot easier once she had a job wish list beside her. She finally felt better and realized that she could find a job to suit her.

Gina breaks the code

Gina didn't like carrying a chip on her shoulder toward her brother. The family was shrinking and she wanted to maintain good relationships with her remaining kin. She told herself that if she was feeling hurt, her brother probably was as well. She decided to speak up about it. She called her brother and after their usual small talk asked, "Do you miss Mom? I sure do." Travis mumbled something and then said, "Mom would turn over in her grave if she saw how you were wasting her hard-earned money." Initially Gina wanted to strike back, but she took a deep breath and said, "Travis, you sound really angry and hurt. Do you want to tell me what's going on?" Travis blurted, "It's not fair. You have a rich husband so you can play with the money from Mom's estate. You've gotten everything you wanted your entire life, while I have to scrimp and save to pay the essentials. Mom and Dad spoiled you rotten, and now your husband spoils you."

Gina didn't like what she heard, but she was glad that Travis was saying what he thought and felt instead of sniping at her. "Travis, I'm sorry you are so hurt and hate me so much. I don't think you have an accurate picture of my circumstances, but if you would like to know me better, I would be happy to answer any questions you have about my finances and my lifestyle. You're my brother and I love you, and I hate to see you so unhappy."

Although Travis and Gina had a long way to go to improve their relationship, Gina's efforts at understanding and listening to Travis' hurt feelings were a step forward. Getting the real issues out on the table was a step toward reconciliation.

Gavin breaks the code

When he reviewed the chart on how to encourage someone who believes him- or herself to be incapable, Gavin focused on the phrase, "Don't give up on her." He had given up on June and was doing everything for her. He'd forgotten how determined she could be when she made up her mind to do something. He didn't think he had caused the current situation, but he was sure he wasn't encouraging June by treating her like she was helpless. Maybe if he did activities with June instead of for her, their situation would improve.

Gavin began by inviting June to sit down with a cup of tea and visit with him in the kitchen while he cooked. Eventually he asked her to help cut vegetables or read steps of a recipe aloud as he worked. He asked her to walk their long driveway with him to retrieve the mail. He said to her, "Honey, it's fun cooking and walking with you. I've missed the woman who landscaped the front yard single-handedly two years ago. You didn't know a thing about gardening when you tackled that. Lately you haven't been yourself." June grinned and said, "I forgot about that person, too. Thanks for reminding me. I guess I felt so overwhelmed by all there is to do around here, that I decided to quit before I started anything else. Do you think we could work together more often? I really don't like doing projects alone."

You can't always make relationships better

There are situations where you will not be able to heal or improve a relationship. If someone is unavailable or unwilling to communicate with respect, refuses to consider his or her behavior, won't cooperate or solve problems, and doesn't make an effort, your only option is to encourage yourself. Encouragement is not a tool to manipulate others into doing what you want them to do. Rather, it's a way to influence the atmosphere in your relationships, which in turn invites (but does not guarantee) healthy interactions. Some people don't want to change, no matter how encouraging you are.

If you say how you feel, ask for what you want, and listen without criticizing, you will feel better, even if it doesn't improve your relationship. Separating yourself physically can help you ignore a bid for undue attention. It can also help you avoid engaging in a power struggle, and stop from retaliating in a discouraged attempt at justice. It can give you time to think and restore your faith in the other when he or she is trying to convince you to give up on him or her. Deciding what you will do to take care of your own needs, setting your limits, and being kind (and firm) are proactive responses to any mistaken behavior. Even if you can't positively impact one relationship, you will be practicing skills that will help you in many other situations.

It may seem like discouraged people calculate and premeditate their behavior to meet relationship needs in useless ways. This is not what we intend. Until you raise your awareness by working through this book, you are not conscious of the purpose of behavior. Now that you know that everything people do is goal-directed, you can catch yourself when using counterproductive means to achieve universal human goals, and you can shift to being encouraging to yourself and to others.

Creating changes in your world

Friends, family members, workshop participants, students, and clients have all told us that once they understood that behavior was not caused by feelings, circumstances, or events, it permanently changed how they viewed their interactions with others.

Changing your behavior to be more encouraging is labor-intensive and doesn't happen without practice. The following are suggestions that will alert you to when you unwittingly sabotage your progress.

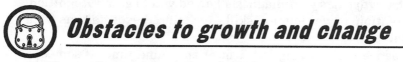

Obstacles to growth and change

1. If your first response is to look for causes or to give yourself or someone else a label, diagnosis, or explanation for behavior, you might not stop to analyze the purpose of that behavior—it's too much work.

2. If you tend to search for a quick fix in any situation, it will be hard for you to work toward more encouraging ways of treating yourself and others who "misbehave." It's less work to react the way you always have when you get certain feelings.

3. If you're attached to proving that you're right and another person is wrong, to being the boss, to prove that you can't be bossed, to making sure you even the score when you've been hurt or offended, or to convince others not to expect certain behavior from you, perhaps you may find it difficult to accept another way of thinking about your situation.

4. If you have a difficult time identifying your feelings, taking the first step in decoding your behavior will be challenging for you.

5. If you look for ways to encourage someone who is misbehaving, it may be a form of coddling the mischief-maker and you won't be inclined to try the ideas in this chapter.

Easy steps for change

☑ This week, notice when you feel annoyed, angry, upset, or withdrawing from you. Ask yourself what you did, and what your purpose might have been.

☑ From the "Turning discouragement into encouragement" chart on pages 142-143, read the list of options for improving your relationships instead of feeding discouragement. Pick out the ones at which you're already good.

☑ From the same list, choose one item from each goal to try this week.

☑ What's your favorite "diagnosis" of yourself? Is it a chemical imbalance, chronic depression, obsession, computer illiteracy, allergy, socially ineptitude, laziness, or something else? In what ways has your diagnosis helped you to gain recognition, attention, power, justice, skills, or reduced expectations from others?

☑ Practice being loving but firm at the same time. If someone you care about wants you to do something and you don't, say, "I love you, but the answer is no." They will survive and so will you. This is a proactive way of dealing with attention-getting behavior, invitations to power struggles, and guilt trips.

☑ Beware of "helping professionals" who, in response to your physical or emotional problems, give you drugs or a diagnosis and tell you that you are sick, instead of helping you understand why something is problematic for you and giving you the tools to handle it.

☑ When you want to be noticed, appreciated, or complemented for something, tell someone and ask him or her to do that for you. Asking for compliments is direct and respectful, fishing for them is annoying.

☑ Plan special time with the important people in your life so they don't have to pester you for your attention.

☑ Any time you're getting ready to say "I'm sick" or "I forgot," practice saying instead, "I don't (didn't) want to."

☑ When your feelings are hurt, say so.

☑ If something seems too hard, ask someone to wait until you are ready or show you a small step to get started.

 **Activities**

Because our three-step process outlined in this chapter can help you with many different situations, it's the only activity we recommend this week. Think of a situation where you feel irritated, worried, annoyed, angry, frustrated, hurt, disappointed, hopeless, or helpless. Write it down. Then use Step 1 to notice your feelings and discover what goal they indicate. Refer to the chart on page 138. Next, using Step 2, identify what you did when you had the feeling, and ask, "What was the result of my reaction? Write that down. Was your response to the mischief more mischief? Did your reaction help you and others escape discouragement? If not, move on to Step 3 and choose a response from the chart on pages 142-143 that is proactive and encouraging instead of reactive and discouraging. Now you have a plan. Use it the next time the situation occurs to invite encouraged, useful behavior.

 **Week 7**

Think, Feel, and Act Like a New Person

Many people do not take responsibility for their actions, feelings, or behaviors, which seem to happen to them as if by magic. It appears to them that they're victims of circumstance and the best they can do is to hope that others change. The thinking goes like this: The spouse abuser can't change unless his wife stops behaving in ways that make him mad; the mother can't stop going crazy until her child behaves; and the aggressive driver has to make the other guy follow the rules of the road. We wish these people luck...because their plans won't work! As you've already discovered in earlier weeks, therapy doesn't happen by wishing other people would change.

In the introduction to *Do-It-Yourself Therapy*, we said that people do three things: They think, they feel, and they act. Your therapy in Week 7 will be to explore the different ways you can make changes, whether you start with your thoughts, your feelings, or your actions; to learn how the three are interrelated; and to discover which of the three paths—thinking, feeling, and doing—enables you to make changes in your life.

Events don't cause feelings or actions

Think about something that happened to you recently where you felt upset or angry. What did you do? Did you react automatically? Did you say or do something that you later regretted? Were you aware of a thought that started off the process? Before reading this book, you may have thought that the situation caused you to feel angry or upset. Now you know that events are triggers and don't cause feelings and actions, and you have a better idea of the part that unconscious thoughts play. (To learn more about the difference between thoughts and feelings and to see how they interrelate, read *How You Feel Is Up to You* by Gary McKay.)

Understanding that your behaviors and feelings don't happen by accident opens another door in discovering the interconnections between thoughts, feelings, and actions. Take Jessie, for example. She was in a heated argument with her roommate. She thought, "Ron's not listening to me, he doesn't care about what I want." She felt angry and was arguing and yelling. The telephone rang. When she picked up the receiver, she heard her best friend's voice. In that split second, Jessie changed her thoughts, "It's Sue calling about our lunch date tomorrow. How nice." She immediately felt cheery and friendly. Her actions changed from hostility to friendliness and her tone of voice reflected her changed attitude. When she got off the phone, Jessie felt angry again and resumed her argument with Ron. How is this quick switch possible?

To answer this question, you have to understand where feelings come from and how they create actions. Most people think that feelings appear spontaneously—that they are caused by external events. One minute you're fine and then the next thing you know, you're angry, excited, sad, hurt, or anxious.

What actually occurs is that you instantly form a thought in response to what happens, often without realizing it. However, events don't cause your thoughts or your feelings, they trigger a pattern of thinking, feeling, and action responses. Although your thoughts might not be in your conscious awareness, they generate your feelings. You can't have a feeling without a thought, and you can't have behavior without a feeling.

Sandra's story

Sandra had problems with her older sister, Sue Ellen, for years. Sandra's therapist suggested that she attend a workshop on relationships, and she agreed to go. When Ari, the workshop facilitator, asked for a volunteer to help him demonstrate the connection between thoughts, feelings, and actions, Sandra raised her hand.

Ari asked Sandra to think about a relationship that was troubling her and to describe it to the group. She started to cry, and Ari reassured her that it was fine to cry and the group would wait until she was ready to tell her story. Between sobs she told the group about the latest occurrence with her sister, who had decided, without involving Sandra, to change the family traditions for Thanksgiving and Christmas. "I feel like she erased me, as usual," she told the group. "I was so upset, I couldn't even finish the conversation, so I hung up on her and haven't stopped crying since."

Ari reassured Sandra and the group that this was a perfect place to help her with her situation. When Sandra calmed down, he asked, "What is it you want in this situation? Knowing your goal will give more meaning to this process." "What I really want is to be part of the decision if there are going to be changes," Sandra replied.

Ari drew three circles on the board to help everyone understand what had happened with Sandra, how what she thought about the problem impacted her feelings and how her feelings affected how she behaved in the situation. He labeled the first circle "think," the second one "feel," and the third "do." Below the circles he wrote, "Sandra's Goal: to be part of the decision-making process."

THINK   FEEL   DO

Sandra's Goal: to be part of the decision-making process

Ari then asked Sandra how she was feeling when Sue Ellen told her that she had changed the holiday plans. Sandra replied, "I wanted to explode." Ari explained to the group and Sandra that "I wanted to explode" was a thought, not a feeling, and asked Sandra to try again. "In one word, how do you feel when you want to explode?" Sandra thought for a moment and replied, "furious." Ari wrote furious in the middle circle.

THINK   FEEL   DO

Sandra's Goal: to be part of the decision-making process

Next, Ari had Sandra describe what she did when she felt furious. Sandra said, "I started to cry," and Ari wrote that in the last circle.

Sandra's Goal: to be part of the decision-making process

"So, you felt furious and you cried. What were you thinking when this happened? What were the thoughts inside your head?" Ari asked. Sandra looked stumped and said, "I don't know." "Most people initially respond like this, because they're not aware of thinking anything. Their thinking isn't happening on a conscious level. Go back to the situation with your sister, concentrate on what thoughts were in your mind, and tell that to me." Sandra paused for a moment and said, "I can't believe she's doing this to me. I don't count." Ari wrote that in the first circle.

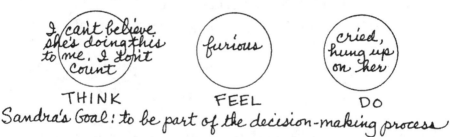

Sandra's Goal: to be part of the decision-making process

"Look at Sandra's pattern," Ari said. "She thinks she's not important, feels furious, and cries. Does this work well in Sandra's life?" Both Sandra and the group members laughed. "It certainly doesn't get me to my goal of being included," Sandra said.

To illustrate how Sandra could create a different, more satisfying pattern, Ari drew three more circles below the original ones, labeled them the same way, and said, "Since you created the first pattern, you can create a new one, which will bring you closer to your goal."

Sandra's Goal: to be part of the decision-making process

Then he asked Sandra what feeling she'd like to feel instead of furious. She thought for a moment and shook her head, saying, "I don't know." Ari showed her the chart of feeling words found on page 169 and explained, "When you're not accustomed to using words for our feelings, it's often difficult to find the right one. This chart will help." Sandra took the chart, looked at it for a minute and pointed to the word calm. Ari wrote "calm" in the middle circle.

"If you were feeling calm," he asked, "What would you be doing?" Sandra replied, "Speak slowly, using regular tone of voice, saying what I want." Ari wrote down what Sandra said in the last circle.

"Now picture yourself feeling calm, speaking in a normal tone of voice.

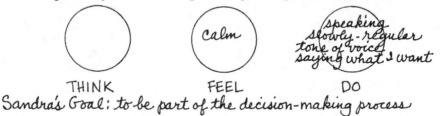

What would you be thinking?" Once again, Sandra paused and then said, "I can deal with her. I can say what I want." He filled in the first circle.

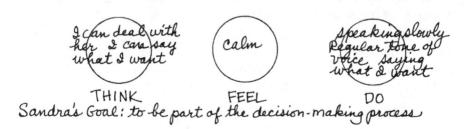

"You've created a different pattern, Sandra. Will this help you reach your goal?" Sandra nodded.

You can create a new pattern for yourself by changing what you think, what you feel or what you do (Activity 1 on page 185-186 walks you through this process to help you make changes in one of your relationships). You can decide how you'd like to feel, what you'd like to do differently, or what you'd rather be telling yourself. As long as you make a change in one circle, the rest of the circles will be different as well. For some of you it will be easier to change your thoughts. Others will need to start with their feelings. Some of you make changes best by learning what to do differently. It makes no difference where you start, as long as you can discover which will be your key path. You may already know which approach is best for you, but if you don't, you're sure to identify it as you read the rest of Week 7.

Unlocking difficulties in relationships

It's not enough to know which path is best for you if you are working on relationship problems. If you try to use logic to work out relationship problems with a person who only changes by focusing on his or her feelings, you could become easily frustrated. Dirk and Paula's story below perfectly illustrates the difficulties of creating a win/win solution between people who make changes differently.

Dirk and Paula's story

Dirk and Paula had a long history of sexual dissatisfaction. Dirk spent hours telling Paula what he wanted in a good sexual relationship. Hardly a day went by when he didn't say something like, "A good sexual relationship brings pleasure and a mutual desire for intimacy. Good sex should be fun, something we can laugh and joke about." The more Dirk "lectured," the less interested Paula was. She would find ways to avoid both the discussion and the practice as much as possible. Dirk couldn't understand what he was doing wrong. Wasn't his attitude about sex respectful, balanced, and cooperative? If Paula told him what she wanted and he could do it for her within reason, he would. He wondered why couldn't Paula act more like a partner.

What Dirk didn't understand was that Paula responded when people asked her about her feelings and listened without judging or correcting her. Although Dirk could describe what he wanted, he wasn't able to hear how Paula was feeling. When she attempted to tell him that she felt embarrassed by her body as she was getting older, or that she was angry because Dirk didn't seem to accept her for who she was, he replied, "That's ridiculous. Your body is just fine and of course I appreciate you." Dirk didn't have a clue what Paula needed. Paula felt that he was "dense" and "uncaring" about her needs.

Dirk had a picture-perfect idea of a fulfilling sexual relationship and couldn't understand why Paula wouldn't want that. He was trying to create change for them by sharing his thoughts and waiting for her to see the light, but his lectures were not getting the desired results. Paula needed Dirk to hear her feelings and not tell her what he wanted. Both ended up disappointed and unsatisfied. They were in a classic power struggle that both were losing. They needed to learn which of the paths to change would be most effective for each of them.

Taking the thinking path to change

The thinking path leads you to working with your beliefs about yourself, others, and the world, some of which are conscious and many of which are subconscious. These beliefs are part of the private logic you began to formulate as a child. They're stored in your brain and come into play automatically as you experience life. Your thoughts are your reality and everyone's thoughts are different. Your unique thoughts are what you think—those are your separate reality. You learned a lot about separate realities in Week 5, but we'd like to expand on the information here to give you additional tools.

Separate realities

To understand separate realities better, picture yourself with the four people standing in a lift line at a ski hill in the picture above. What would you be thinking?

Notice that each person has thoughts that are unique and separate from all the others. The closer your thoughts are to someone else's, the fewer problems you'll have with him or her. If you didn't know about separate realities, you'd probably believe that everyone was thinking what you are thinking, and you wouldn't consider checking in to find out what was on other people's minds.

When people bring separate realities into their relationships and get locked into "right or wrong" thinking, the situation often turns into a battleground and change doesn't happen. Problems result if you don't comprehend, value, and treat differences with respect. There isn't a person alive who hasn't experienced this type of difficulty. Developing an attitude of curiosity, as well as becoming aware of emotional baggage are two ways to handle differences that can create closeness instead of conflict.

Developing an attitude of curiosity

When you develop an attitude of curiosity, you are able to explore someone else's view of reality in a nonthreatening way. A curious attitude allows you to remain open, to get information, to learn about the other person, to care, and to understand the other person's issues. Practice being curious as a way of building a bridge between your reality and someone else's. Think how much better the situation might have been between Dirk and Paula, the couple with the intimacy issues, had one of them had an attitude of curiosity.

Jamie and Nadia's story

Jamie and Nadia were friends who met to exercise together once a week. Nadia complained that Jamie ran too fast and wanted her to go slower. Jamie couldn't understand what the problem was. She never

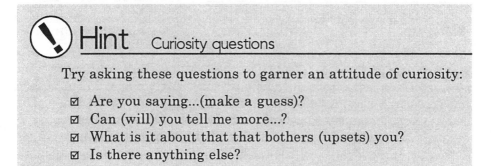

Hint Curiosity questions

Try asking these questions to garner an attitude of curiosity:

- ☑ Are you saying...(make a guess)?
- ☑ Can (will) you tell me more...?
- ☑ What is it about that that bothers (upsets) you?
- ☑ Is there anything else?

complained about how slowly Nadia ran, and she didn't mind waiting for her in the parking lot at the end of their run. In fact, she encouraged Nadia to go at a pace that was comfortable for her, but telling Nadia this only resulted in an argument.

Jamie knew they weren't seeing things eye-to-eye, so she decided to practice an attitude of curiosity to see what she could learn. After a bit of small talk over coffee, she asked Nadia, "What did you mean the other day when you said to me, 'You think you're so fast?' " Nadia answered, "We meet to run together and then you take off." "Are you saying that I run faster than you?" Jamie asked. "Of course you do. You just start out and leave me." "Tell me more," Jamie said. "My idea of exercising together is running side-by-side so we can talk. I don't like ending up alone," Nadia answered. "What is it about that upsets you?" Jamie asked. "I don't enjoy running unless I have someone to talk with, and I especially don't like to run in the park alone. It scares me. I think it's safer if there are two of us," Nadia responded. "Now I get it," Jamie said. "I'm glad I asked, because I wouldn't have guessed that bothers you," Jamie said.

What Jamie discovered by adopting a curious attitude was that they each had a different picture of their exercise time together. Both were right in their ideas. Nadia wanted to run together. Jamie liked being out, each running at a pace that was comfortable, meeting at the end.

If Jamie and Nadia want to come up with a plan that will work for both of them, it will help if they give up trying to change each other and just accept that their thinking is different. Picture yourself in a similar situation. Could you be open to suggestion, instead of looking for blame, trying to prove one of you is right and the other is wrong?

Discovering your personal baggage

Another way you can discover how you think differently than others is to examine your baggage. Picture yourself packing a suitcase full of the ideas and conclusions you formed when you were young. You carry it with you throughout your life. Now you operate in an adult body in an adult world, pulling ideas from the suitcase, and using your childhood reasoning. You carry these beliefs and old messages around like baggage. (This is based on workshop material by Maxime Ijams as presented in *To Know Me Is to Love Me* by Lott, Kentz, and West.)

You can have baggage about any issue: money, education, sex, men, women, work, children, vacations, religion, illness, marriage, love, politics, and more. In relationships you'll find that when your baggage is similar to the other person's about certain issues, you'll experience less stress in these areas. When your baggage is different, you'll experience conflict and may not realize why. You might think the other person is being stubborn or giving you a hard time until you accept that your realities are different.

If you'd like to become aware of the baggage you carry with you, make a list of any of the issues listed above that concern you. Feel free to add other topics of importance to you. Look at the issue and write down whatever comes to your mind. If you don't know what to write, think about the messages you got on that subject as you were growing up. Sometimes it helps to imagine a sign hanging in your childhood home that makes some statement about the issue.

To understand how your individual baggage is important in your relationships, notice how Bart and Blake's baggage creates problems.

When Bart and Blake compared their lists, it was obvious for the first time why they fought so much. They wondered what attracted them to each other in the first place. If you are dealing with a relationship issue, compare your list of baggage with the other person's if he or she is willing. Identify some origins of harmony or discord in your relationship. Hopefully you will have more areas of compatibility than Blake and Bart. If you avoid thinking in absolutes, you and the other person may come up with some solutions, or at least, understand and accept your differences.

Giving up magical thinking

Paying attention to how much you and others indulge in magical thinking is another way to make changes. If you're unhappy in a relationship and you keep hoping everything will get better, you are engaging in magical thinking. If Blake and Bart thought all their differences would dissolve if they waited long enough, that would be magical thinking. When you practice magical thinking, you prevent yourself from seeing reality. If you don't know the difference between fantasy and reality, you can't make healthy choices. Magical thinking only brings you disappointment. Notice how magical thinking creates chaos in the following relationships.

Annette's story

Annette had been married to Chuck for 12 years. They had three children and lived in the countryside, as Annette had dreamed she would one day. Unfortunately, that was the only way Annette's reality matched her dreams. The husband in her fantasy was kind, playful, and loving. However, her *real* husband worked all day, came home exhausted just before the children's bedtime, and yelled at them for being messy and irresponsible. His constant criticisms were abusive. On one occasion he pushed Annette into a wall when she begged him not to yell at the children. Annette's friends urged her to leave before her situation got worse, but she told them her family was important and the situation would get better as soon as Chuck was less stressed at work. Annette's magical thinking kept her living in the past or hoping for a better future.

Arnie's story

Arnie believed that saying something made it happen. For example, if he wanted to remodel his kitchen, he could picture completing the job in his mind. So when the work wasn't done in reality, he wondered why his wife complained—he *said* he'd remodel the kitchen.

This form of magical thinking drove a lot of people crazy—especially at his office. He constantly made promises he didn't keep. When someone called him on his lack of follow-through, he would look genuinely confused and say, "I could have sworn I did that already. Didn't I say that I would?"

Why did Annette insist on staying in an abusive relationship? Why did Arnie believe he could tell people what they wanted to hear and that would be enough? As long as Annette was living with her husband and children, she could hold onto the fantasy that she had a wonderful family, house, and marriage. As long as Arnie believed his own words, he could avoid taking responsibility for his behavior. What would it take for Annette or Arnie to come to terms with reality? For Annette, being physically abused, seeing her children hurt, or finding out that Chuck was having an affair might serve as a wake-up call. For Arnie, getting fired might get his attention.

Don't wait until your life deteriorates to give up your magical thinking. Start by noticing the increased stress you feel. Stress can indicate that the distance between your ideal and reality has widened. Ask yourself what reality you are avoiding with magical thinking? How would your life be different if you accepted reality? Whatever it is, have the confidence that you can handle it. You'll have the opportunity to turn disappointment into happiness if you stop indulging in magical thinking. You can replace old, destructive thoughts with new ideas by facing your current reality. Believing that you can change your thinking is the first step forward. This is only one way to give yourself an attitude adjustment. There are many more.

Giving yourself an attitude adjustment

You've heard the expression, "You are what you eat." Well, we've changed it to, "You are what you think." You know people who have a pessimistic, negative, "poor me" attitude, who always see the cup half empty. They don't seem satisfied or have what they want in relationships and life. Yet, they seem totally unaware of how their attitude may be inviting the responses they get. How do you respond to people with chips on their shoulders? Do you want to spend a lot of time with them, or do you keep your distance? On the other hand, people who have an optimistic, positive attitude see the cup half full. They invite very different responses. How do you respond to these people?

Are you optimistic or pessimistic? To help you determine whether you might need an attitude adjustment, take a few minutes and get in touch with your current frame of mind. Do you see the cup as half empty or half full? How is this reflected in your life? Do others call you negative? Do you approach each day with energy and excitement or would you rather stay in bed? Do you complain about everyone and everything? If you're not sure how to answer these questions, ask a friend what he or she notices about you. Your friend may be more objective about how you come across. Once you are aware of your attitude, you can give yourself an attitude adjustment by changing how you think.

Pierre's story

Pierre entered a treatment facility after his wife packed her things, took their four-year-old daughter, and moved out. She had spent the last year attending Al-Anon meetings because she was concerned about his drinking, and his arrest for driving under the influence (DUI) was the last straw. As they were walking out the door, Pierre's daughter looked at him and said, "Daddy, you drink too much." Her words broke Pierre's heart.

At first, when he was in treatment, Pierre didn't think that his drinking was much of a problem. After all, he thought, he didn't drink as much as most of his buddies. In fact, he was always the one who drove his friends home—that's how he got the DUI. But as he spent more time in the treatment facility, Pierre began to see the devastating effects that alcohol had in his life. His father had been a violent drunk who beat his children. Pierre thought that since he never behaved like his father had, he wasn't so bad. As he talked in group he began to realize how often he hadn't been there for his wife and daughter and how much he had cut himself off from his feelings.

When he finished the program, Pierre continued with AA meetings daily, got a sponsor, attended his aftercare group, and diligently worked his recovery program. He pleaded with his wife to come home and promised that life would be different. She had heard his promises before and knew that she wanted more time, and that she needed to pay attention to his actions and not his words.

As Pierre worked through AA, his attitude and approach to life changed. He stopped drinking and now he thought about how he wanted his life to be. He shared his feelings and began talking to his wife about the things that bothered him. Life wasn't perfect but Pierre felt himself growing. At a meeting where he received his one-year chip, he said, with tears in his eyes, "I never thought I'd say this, but I'm a grateful alcoholic and now I truly know what that means."

Treatment and recovery were the road to Pierre's attitude adjustment. In the process of reading this book, you've already discovered many ways to change your attitude.

Rewriting your beliefs

We suggest this activity for those of you who make changes by working with your thoughts. If you prefer making changes using your feelings or actions, you will find the other options for change more helpful. (We were shown this helpful practice by our colleague Lee Schnebly.) Start by writing out a list of your beliefs, cross off the parts you don't like, and rewrite new decisions in their places. To help you create belief statements you can use this week, return to Week 5 where you wrote out your early memories and discovered how to interpret them and uncover your beliefs.

When you work with your memories, look for the extremes in your thinking, statements that imply there is only one way things can be. See if you can come up with more encouraging alternatives. When you

complete your list, put it up where you can look at it daily. These can become affirmations for you. In the hint box below, notice how each person
changed a belief to create more moderate, encouraging, and empowering
statements for him- or herself. Remember Harry, Shane, Blythe, and Don
from Week 5? They all rewrote their belief statements below. Take a look
to see how they turned discouragement into encouragement:

> *I don't have to do it by myself—I can ask for help.*
> **Harry:** I ~~can't let anybody help~~ me.
>
> 　　　*can*　　　　　　　　*if I want it.*
> **Shane:** I ~~won't~~ ask for help ~~anymore~~.
>
> 　　　*and I don't have to worry that I am second-rate.*
> **Blythe:** I love being included, ~~and not treated as second-rate~~.
>
> 　　　*that I've made a mistake and it's not the end of the world.*
> **Dom:**　　I see what I've done and know ~~I'm in trouble now~~.

Changing thinking with affirmations

You can make a list of affirmations for yourself in other ways. There
are many books, calendars, journals, and other tools with daily thoughts

---

! **Hint**　Rewriting your beliefs

Here are some examples on how to rewrite your beliefs:

　　can have a　　*and speak up for myself.*
1. I ~~have no~~ voice.

　　sometimes like to be　　　　*but I can share the stage*
2. I ~~have to be~~ the center of attention.

　　can't
3. Others ~~can~~ dominate me.

　　will listen to me when I share my point of view.
4. Others ~~don't listen or ask for my point of view~~.

　　can be fair.
5. Life ~~is unfair~~.

　　(no change needed)
6. Life is hopeful.

and words of wisdom. If you communicate by e-mail, you probably receive a list of affirmations from someone at least once a week. Affirmations are a popular method for changing your thinking by replacing old, destructive patterns of thought with new, optimistic, affirming ones.

Once you find a source of affirmations you like, make a list for yourself. Stick it on your bathroom mirror, refrigerator, or some place where you can read it every day. The more you read and surround yourself with your affirmations, the quicker they will become part of your thinking.

Taking the feeling path to change

As Adlerians we believe that we are indivisible beings, that our minds and our bodies are connected, and that our beliefs impact our physiology. We have come across many clients who express their issues through their bodies; changes don't happen for them until they work with their bodies to access their feelings. If you are a person who prefers the feeling path to change, you will find help in this section of Week 7.

Learning from your illnesses

Another way to follow the feeling path to change is to learn from your illnesses. If you feel ill, you probably find a doctor who looks for

---

(!) Hint   Affirmations to help you get started

- ☑ Challenge yourself.
- ☑ If you keep doing what you're doing, you'll keep on getting what you're getting.
- ☑ "Follow your bliss and doors will open where there were no doors before." —Joseph Campbell
- ☑ Adventures don't begin until you get into the forest.
- ☑ "That first step is an act of faith." —Mickey Hart
- ☑ Others will listen to me.
- ☑ I am 100-percent responsible for what happens to me.
- ☑ I deserve to be happy.
- ☑ "Keep an open mind." —Alcoholics Anonymous
- ☑ "Progress, not perfection" —Alcoholics Anonymous
- ☑ "One day at a time." —Alcoholics Anonymous

the cause or diagnoses a disease. He or she then attempts to cure or control it using methods such as surgery, radiation, or medication. We, on the other hand, have another way of understanding illness. We encourage you to discover what purpose the ailment may be serving, so you can see options for taking an active part in your healing.

Illness can serve a purpose. If you are experiencing "dis-ease," you feel uncomfortable, in distress, and in pain. You don't get sick on purpose; ailments are real, and sometimes even fatal. But illness serves a purpose, in that your body "speaks" to you. You may even use expressions that reflect the notion of body talk like: "She's a pain in the neck," "Get off my back," and "He doesn't shoulder responsibility."

A few of the most obvious purposes for illness may be to gain recognition by being the person who is always sick. You may look to get special service by having others care for you. Or you may wish to be excused from certain tasks or aspects of life. For example, missing a day of work because you need a break may not be acceptable, while staying home because you are "sick" is allowed.

It's not conscious or intentional, but once you understand the purpose of an illness, you can decide what you want to do about it and

---

(!) Hint   Methods to help you access your feelings

- ☑ Massage, Rolfing, and other forms of body work.
- ☑ Acupressure.
- ☑ Acupuncture.
- ☑ Chiropractory.
- ☑ Meditation.
- ☑ Guided imagery and hypnosis.
- ☑ Biofeedback.
- ☑ Exercise, jogging, walking, working out at a gym...
- ☑ Sports such as swimming, skiing, skating, tennis...
- ☑ Yoga.
- ☑ T'ai chi or martial arts.
- ☑ Dancing: ballroom, modern, tap, jazz, folk, square...
- ☑ Art therapy.
- ☑ Psychodrama and other drama activities.
- ☑ Healthy eating.

whether you want to participate in your healing process by exploring other constructive ways to get your needs met.

Our thinking here isn't unique. Many people have recognized the body/mind connection and used it to help others heal. (Specifically, we appreciate the work of Louise Hay, and find her book, *Heal Your Body* invaluable in our work with clients.)

Karen's story

Karen and her husband Joe, who recently passed his CPA exam, were newly married and starting out in Denver. They looked up a friend they heard lived in town. Marnie had married a doctor and was already well-established. Delighted to hear from her old friends, she invited Karen and Joe to a dinner party at her home. When they arrived for dinner, Karen and Joe saw several Cadillacs, Mercedes, and BMWs parked in front. The conversation revolved around investments and property. By the time the maid served dinner, Karen and Joe found themselves feeling very uncomfortable.

Karen thought she should reciprocate and invited Marnie and her husband to dinner a few weeks later. As the day neared, Karen was feeling anxious. The day before the dinner, while Karen was vacuuming, she bent over and suddenly she couldn't move. For the very first time in her life, her back had gone out. She called Joe to take her to the doctor. After a cortisone shot and a bottle of muscle relaxants, she called her friends and apologetically canceled the dinner.

Years later, Karen realized what had happened. She had decided that she was outclassed and felt so uncomfortable that she couldn't go through with having her friends over for dinner. Since this wouldn't have been an appropriate reason to cancel dinner, Karen unconsciously created an acceptable way to excuse herself, even though it meant she ended up in excruciating pain. Had Karen understood that unreleased feelings can end up wreaking havoc in her body, she may have chosen a less-complicated approach to her problem and told her friend the truth.

Martin's story

Martin worked at a body shop after he graduated from high school. Although he enjoyed working on cars, he detested his boss. He hated being ordered around, criticized, and being kept late, only to hear complaints about overtime pay.

Martin stopped by his mother's house after a particularly difficult day at work and said, "I can't take it anymore." His mother suggested he talk to his boss, as he really needed the job and a new one might be hard to find. Martin was afraid of his boss, but after talking to his mother, he decided he'd give it a try. The next morning Martin woke up with laryngitis. His voice was nothing but a squeak, so he decided to stay home.

Bonnie's story

Bonnie found it extremely difficult to be outside, because she was allergic to grasses, weeds, and just about everything that grew. Even with medications, she sneezed, wheezed, and itched. One day she was in a class on Adlerian Psychology, and the topic was purposes of behavior. Bonnie was aware that she really hated doing yard work and she wondered if there was a connection between this and her allergies. She decided to do an experiment to find out. Her first step was to mentally change her "I can'ts" to "I don't want to's." Then she gathered her courage and told her husband aloud one day, "I don't want to do yard work," instead of, "I can't because of my allergies." Over time Bonnie noticed that she needed less medication and could be outdoors without major discomfort. She also discovered that her husband was happy to do the yard work if she didn't mind taking the car to the car wash and doing the shopping.

⚠ Hint   Unconscious thoughts and physical conditions

Was Martin's laryngitis a coincidence? Look at some of the unconscious thoughts that could be underlying other physical conditions as addressed in Louise Hay's book, *Heal Your Body*. Do any of these fit for you?

- ☑ **Lower backache:** Fear of money. Lack of financial support.
- ☑ **Upper backache:** Lack of emotional support. Feeling unloved. Holding back love.
- ☑ **Headaches:** Invalidating the self. Self-criticism. Fear.
- ☑ **Kidney stones:** Lumps of undissolved anger.
- ☑ **Snoring:** Stubborn refusal to give up old patterns.
- ☑ **Sore throat:** Holding in angry words. Feeling unable to express the self.

Learning more about your feelings

We have said that feelings are energy in your body. Some of you may have trouble recognizing that the energy inside your body is a feeling. Perhaps you have referred to this energy as indigestion or some other condition. You might also refer to your feelings using sentences that start with "I feel like," "I feel that you," or "I feel as if." But whatever words come after "like," "that you," and "as if" are thoughts, not feelings. Maybe you recognize that you are having a feeling, but you have difficulty naming it. Few people have a feeling vocabulary, which is why we include the "Feelings Chart" for you on the next page. Post the chart on your refrigerator to help you recognize the words that go with feelings.

Many of you grew up believing that having certain kinds of feelings were bad. Feelings are neither right nor wrong, good nor bad, positive nor negative—they simply tell you about something that's going on inside you. It's fine to have whatever feelings you have. Don't judge them and don't be afraid to experience and express them. Once you learn to pay attention to feelings and name them, you'll discover a lot of valuable information about yourself. Your feelings never lie to you. You may be afraid to identify them because you think that then you'll have to do something about or with them. But feelings are different from behavior. Although they are energy, you have many choices about what to do when you have a feeling. Perhaps, like Anna in the following story, you didn't know that you had choices.

Anna's story

Anna didn't understand why, sometimes, she would suddenly want to "kill" the person next to her for what he or she just did or said. Of course, she didn't murder anyone, but she did yell, scream, and lash out. At other times she'd sit stone-faced and silent, hoping no one would notice. Anna found it difficult to recognize or admit that she was having a feeling, that the name for it was "angry," or that it was okay for her or anyone else to have that feeling.

Like many, Anna had no experience dealing with feelings productively or respectfully. Instead, she used the energy from her anger to attack or withdraw. She grew up in a situation where others excused their behavior when they were angry by saying, "Sorry, I lost my temper." But if they had really lost their tempers, they wouldn't have them anymore. It would be more accurate to say that they used their tempers, like Anna, by screaming at the people around them.

We emphasize that you deal with your feelings in respectful ways. When you are angry, it's not okay to hurt someone else, hurt yourself, or hurt property. Constructive and appropriate expressions of anger aren't the same as displays that have the purpose of intimidating, overpowering, threatening, or distancing from others. Ask yourself, when you are having a feeling, "What purpose does this feeling serve? Am I using it to intimidate someone, to win, to touch another's heart, to create distance, to achieve closeness, to avoid something, to get attention, to give myself permission, to create pain, to stop myself, to create intimacy, to (you fill in the blank)? What is this feeling for?"

Anna could be afraid of her anger, because of the frightening displays she's witnessed. Anger, like many other feelings, has a bad reputation. Every feeling is attempting to tell you something you need to know. For instance, anger tells you you're not getting something that you want or need, or that you're in a power struggle. Depression tells you that your attitudes and your life need serious readjusting so your ideals and your realities can move closer together. Jealousy is a goal-setting feeling that tells you what is important to you and what you want. Boredom is a feeling that signals you're ready for a change. You can use it to rest, brainstorm, and look for something inspiring, before moving out of the transition boredom provides you.

Reed's story

Reed, a well-liked family practice doctor, had been feeling depressed for about eight months. He'd stopped jogging, hated going to work, and when he came home, he complained constantly about all the reports he had to write. His department head never missed an opportunity to reprimand him because he wasn't getting patients in and out fast enough or keeping up with the paperwork. Reed didn't like being admonished, threatened, or told he couldn't give his patients the time and attention he felt they deserved.

Reed felt additional pressure because he and his wife had recently bought a house and they liked living in town. On the one hand, he was afraid he'd have to move if he lost his job, but on the other hand, he couldn't stand having to practice medicine this way. He felt trapped, discouraged, and depressed and even had thoughts of ending it all, although he didn't think he'd actually kill himself.

We know that some people have periodic "bouts" with depression and some have felt depressed for years. They have been in unhappy or abusive relationships at home or at work. They develop a constellation of thoughts, feelings, and behaviors that become a paralyzing discouragement. If they listen carefully to their feeling of depression instead of medicating it, they will realize that the feeling is telling them to do something to improve their situation.

When Reed listened to his feelings, he decided to start therapy. In therapy, he discovered that his department head reminded him of his violent and abusive father, who would burst into a room, grab the closest child, and beat him. Reed had no way of protecting himself or his brothers, any more than he could when his department head randomly rebuked and threatened him. It's no wonder he felt depressed. However, Reed realized he was no longer a child and that he wasn't trapped. He had choices and he was ready to take action.

Mitch's story

Whenever Mitch went over to his sister's house to visit, her boyfriend was always there, sitting close, kissing her on the couch. Mitch felt uncomfortable. He told his friend Judy about this, and she looked at him and said, "You sound jealous." "I am not," Mitch shot back. "Wait a minute, Mitch, it's not a crime. Jealousy is a feeling that tells you what you want. Didn't you tell me that you wished you had someone special in your life?"

Mitch could spend more time meeting people, participating in activities with like-minded souls, writing a personal ad, or telling his friends he'd like to be introduced to more women. Instead of beating yourself up for feeling jealous, use this feeling to figure out how to go about getting what you want.

Pamela's story

Pamela found herself feeling bored and restless when her youngest child graduated from high school and went off to college. She'd heard about "the empty nest," but was sure it would never be an issue for her, because she'd been counting the days until she could do all the things on her "what I'll get to do when I'm childless" list. Now the day had come, and she was feeling bored and wasn't doing much of anything. She had thought that what she really wanted to do was go back to school, but that seemed really frightening—she was sure it was too late. As the deadline for registration came closer, Pamela began to have nightmares. She dreamt about monsters that visited her and scared her. She didn't understand what this meant so she decided to talk about her dreams in a women's group.

The facilitator asked Pamela to imagine she was in her dream, turn around and face her monsters, pretend they were her friends, and ask them what they were trying to tell her and why they had to scare her to get her attention. "They're telling me I'm too old, it's too late, I'm not smart enough, school's too hard, everyone else will be younger, and I'm too old to start a new career even if I do graduate. I guess I'm really scared and I'm stopping myself from doing anything. No wonder I'm bored."

Another group member told Pamela she had the same feelings and concerns when she went back to school and that she would be happy to walk Pamela through the process. She even offered to meet her for coffee on the campus and show her around. Pamela lit up, realizing that there were some small steps she could take to help her deal with her feelings of boredom and fear. She said, "I didn't realize my feelings were like flashlights to show me the way. I've spent a lifetime trying to ignore them instead of use them."

We hope you will use your feelings like flashlights to light your direction. Instead of avoiding or ignoring your feelings, figure out what they are telling you.

Feel your feelings, don't *think* them!

Even if you believe it's okay to have your feelings, you may be thinking them instead of feeling them, losing out on the help they can give you. We suggest that you use this simple method to help you feel your feelings: Put your hand over your heart or on your stomach before you begin talking. This will help you speak words that come straight from your heart and your gut, not from your head. Try it and see the difference. The more you can speak from your feelings, the more you'll be able to connect with others. Discovering this can be a turning point in your relationships.

Rosa and Miguel's story

Rosa and Miguel's four-year-old son was in a co-op preschool. Rosa attended the weekly evening meetings, while Miguel stayed home with their son. One week, a few of the moms decided to go to a local bar for a drink after the meeting. When Rosa came home and told Miguel how excited she was to be making friends with the other moms, she couldn't understand why he looked so angry, but neither Rosa nor Miguel said anything more that night.

The following weeks, Rosa noticed Miguel was irritable on meeting nights. Before each meeting he questioned her incessantly as to what time she'd be home. He also began to make it difficult for her to get out of the house on time. Rosa asked Miguel what was going on, and he replied, "Nothing." But Rosa knew something was wrong and decided to try what she had learned at her meeting about communication.

She put her hand on her heart and told Miguel she was sad when he acted like he didn't trust her and wanted her to stay home on meeting nights. She moved her hand to her stomach and continued, "I feel upset and resentful and wonder if you don't want me to have friends." Miguel started to tell Rosa how much he had to do at the house, how difficult their son was, and that he didn't think she should have to go to meetings at night.

"Okay, I hear you, but that was from your head," Rosa said. "Now put your hand on your heart and talk to me. I want to hear your feelings." Miguel looked surprised but as she gently held his hand to his heart, he said, "I miss having you here at night. I work hard all day and like to be with you."

"Okay," Rosa responded, "Now put your hand on your gut and tell me what's really going on."

"What do you mean?" Miguel questioned.

"Be honest with me," Rosa replied. "All this started when I told you about going to the bar."

"I hate that you go out to a bar. You are beautiful and I'm afraid some guy will try to pick you up. I'm afraid I could lose you." Rosa realized that under his anger, deep down, Miguel was afraid.

Miguel, like most people, had no trouble talking from his head, living his life from the neck up. To live life from the neck down means moving into your feelings. When you recognize and share your feelings, you begin to speak from your heart and your gut. Moving to a gut level enables you to speak your deepest, most honest feelings. Think of the expression, "gut-level honest." When you can reach this level you are being completely genuine.

Rosa felt compassion for Miguel when he was gut-level honest. She felt his vulnerability and was touched by his desire for her. Gut-level honesty creates true intimacy in a relationship. For you to express your feelings at that level, it helps if you feel safe knowing the other person won't put you down, invalidate you, or make fun of you. At the same time, you invite respect and compassion from the other when you open yourself in that way.

Using dreams to discover your feelings

Your dreams are yet another source of information about your feelings. There are many ways you can work with your dreams to access the information they have for you. However, our focus is on the feelings your dreams create, and how you can use them for constructive change. If you forget your dreams, you might be avoiding dealing with your feelings. If you want to understand better the role your feelings play, keep a pad of paper and pencil at your bedside and write down any dreams you have this week.

Along with giving you valuable messages that can help you in your life, dreams are also factories for creating feelings. With every dream, a feeling is created that can move you forward, backward, or keep you stuck, like in Gloria's story. Some of the other ways to work with dreams include: reenacting your dreams in psychodrama, interpreting symbolic images in your dreams using books, journal-writing to record your dreams, evaluating the parts of your dream to discover what those parts have to say to you, and joining a dream group where other people can tell you what your dream means to them.

Gloria's story

Gloria's daughter Dorothy had recently gotten her driver's license. Dorothy was an excellent driver—responsible, skilled, and careful—so she couldn't understand why her mother was so worried when she wanted to drive to a nearby city to shop and visit the cafes. Gloria, a world-class worrier, pictured the car breaking down, her daughter getting run over while changing a flat, a mugging, a kidnapping, or any other frightening scenario she had seen on TV.

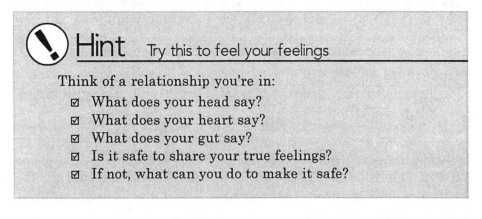

(!) Hint   Try this to feel your feelings

Think of a relationship you're in:

- ☑ What does your head say?
- ☑ What does your heart say?
- ☑ What does your gut say?
- ☑ Is it safe to share your true feelings?
- ☑ If not, what can you do to make it safe?

Dorothy was accustomed to her mother's catastrophizing, and tried to reassure her by agreeing to carry a car phone, bring a friend along, or even take a self-defense course. She was willing to do anything to help her mother handle her fears, but Gloria was unmoved. She knew she was being unreasonable and discouraging, but she couldn't help herself.

That night, Gloria had a dream. In it, she was chasing her daughter down a road, then through a field, then into a house, where she lost her in the maze of rooms. She felt something sticky underfoot, and looked down to notice the floors were dirty. Sidetracked by the mess, she decided to find a mop and clean the floor.

When she woke up, Gloria felt agitated, nervous, and guilty. She realized that she could use the energy from her feelings in one of three ways: to make things worse, to stay stuck, or to improve her situation. To make things worse, all she would have to do would be to become more controlling. Guilt would help her stay stuck; when people feel guilty, it's a sign that they are going to act exactly the same and excuse their previous behavior. Or she could use her feelings to improve her situation by feeling agitated, nervous, and guilty about not letting go—something she knows is necessary with a child this age. When you dream, your feelings don't cause certain actions, but they do give you choices and energy. Like Gloria, it's up to you to decide which direction your actions will take you.

Taking the action path to change

Actions are what you do to make the changes you want. We know you're not a person who spends a lot of time and energy thinking about changes you'd like without doing anything to make them happen because you're reading this book. If you follow the action path to change, you've probably already used many suggestions and activities in the **Creating Changes in Your World** sections each week. For right now, we'll focus on three more ways to make action changes: cleaning up your communication, learning about your love prototype, and creating action plans.

Cleaning up your communication

You can clean up your communication by taking the blame out of your conversation, creating respectful exchanges of feelings that allow for other people's realities. (*See* Week 8 for many other ways to clean up your communication.) Although there are many communication techniques to help you do all of this, we find the formula "I feel...because...and I wish..." to be the most effective. This kind of "I message" is easy to use. It requires few words, so others are more likely to listen instead of tuning you out. It begins with a statement of your feelings, which creates an immediate connection to others. People don't do a good job of guessing how you feel or what you want. If you use this formula, you will be able to share your feelings easily (and respectfully) with others.

We discovered "I messages" for the first time in the work of Thomas Gordon, but it is difficult to use his formula without using the word "you." This puts the listener on the defensive immediately. Lynn came up with the idea of starting with "I feel," followed by a feeling word, as most people will stop what they're doing and listen when someone says a feeling word at the outset.

Faye's story

Faye had an ongoing battle with her roommate about taking the garbage out. Stuart said he wanted to be in charge of garbage, but he never took the trash out unless Faye nagged, yelled, and threatened to do it herself. She decided to try out the "I feel...because..." message and carefully wrote out what she wanted to say. The next time she saw the trash overflowing, she went to Stuart and calmly said, "I feel angry because the trash is overflowing, and I wish you'd empty it now." At first Stuart started to make excuses and Faye calmly repeated, "We have an agreement and I'd like you to keep it." Stuart stammered something unintelligible, grabbed the garbage and headed out the door.

(!) Hint   Your "I feel...because...and I wish" message

1. Start by thinking about what you would like to communicate to someone. Then look at the feeling faces on page 169 to find a feeling word that fits for you.
2. Fill in the following blanks by writing down your thoughts before speaking them:
   I feel (use a feeling word)
   Because (effect of the problem or behavior on you)
   And I'd like (what is it you wish or want?)
3. Say this message to the other person.

Although this format may seem simple, it takes practice to identify your feelings and send a respectful message. We recommend that you do not use the word you, as it invites defensiveness and resistance. Even if you create a perfect "I feel...because..." statement, it's important to remember that just because you ask for what you need or want, doesn't mean you'll get it. You can only do your part. If the other person isn't willing to respond or communicate respectfully in return, then you can decide what you will do.

Using the love prototype

If you don't feel lovable or loved, you cause all kinds of mischief because you're discouraged. The "love prototype" provides a quick way to encourage anyone and give them an injection of that sense of being lovable and loved. It might be the single most useful tool couples discover for getting the message of love across to each other. (we first heard about the love prototype from Gloria Lane at a N.A.S.A.P. convention.)

The family is the first place you learned about love. So much of what you learned occurred before you acquired language or adult logic, that now you act automatically without awareness. Your actions are based on your "prototype" for showing and feeling love; a model you created with your decisions about your early experiences. How you show love and what invites you to feel loved is unique to you. To discover how your love prototype is constructed, write out the answers to the following questions.

1. As a child growing up, how did you show love to your parents (or the adults who were responsible for you)? This may be different for each parent. Write all the ways you showed love to your parents.
2. How did your parents show you love when you were growing up? List all the ways the adults who cared for you showed you love. This may have been different for each of them.
3. If you like, you can ask your friend or partner to answer the same two questions. If your answers include phrases such as "be good" or "be responsible," define what that means more specifically. For example, "be good" might really mean "do my chores on time" or "do what I was asked."
4. Fill in the template on the next page with your answers.

Love prototype template			
	You	**Your Partner**	
♥ **Show love by**	Write in your answers to number 1	Write in your partner's answers to number 2	♥ **Feel love by**
♥ **Feel love by**	Write in your answers to number 2	Write in your partner's answers to number 1	♥ **Show love by**

You now have your model for showing and feeling loved. When you look at the template you filled in, you might notice that you are showing love to someone in a way he or she doesn't feel loved, and vice versa. Now that the information is conscious, ask the other person if he or she could, in addition to what he or she is already doing, show you love according to what makes you feel loved. Doing this exercise can quickly clarify and mend love issues in your relationship.

If you answered "I didn't feel loved," or "I don't remember," it could be that you don't notice when someone is showing love. Or it may mean that you have no model. You can be open to learning ways to feel or show love. The love prototype is one kind of action plan.

Creating an action plan for change

We have identified six steps to help you create an action plan for change. One of the advantages of the action plan is that it helps you create a routine or structure. You might resist the idea of routine, thinking that it will box you in. But we find that routines of your own making can create security and order out of chaos. Another feature of an action plan is that it offers you a way to let go of the old so you can make room for the new. Sometimes it's almost impossible to make changes because there is no room in your life for a new program. To get you started, here are the six steps to our action plan: First, create a picture; second, plan your steps; third, identify your stumbling blocks;

fourth, plan a rehearsal; fifth, follow through with action; and sixth, reevaluate your plan.

Step 1: Create a picture

Some people have a clear picture of what the change they want would look like. Others don't have a clue. Reading this book may have given you some new ideas about changes you'd like to see in your life. But until you have a distinct picture in your mind, it's almost impossible to create what you want. The hint box below offers tips to help you get a picture for yourself.

Step 2: Plan your steps

This is a time to think things through in advance. You can write out your plan for a clearer picture. Decide:

1. Each action step you will take. Spell out exactly what you will do and how. Be brief and limit yourself to no more than four steps.
2. For each step, the time line. When will you do it?
3. For each step, the place. Where will you do it?
4. When you'll reevaluate. Will you give yourself a day? A week?

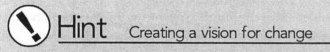

Hint   Creating a vision for change

1. Close your eyes and visualize the change you'd like to create in your relationships. Look at how people are interacting. What do the surroundings look like? Paint this new picture in your mind's eye.
2. Use a magic wand. Think of anything you'd like and indulge yourself in your fantasy. This can help you get unstuck and see new options that you may not have thought of before.
3. Tell a friend about the situation or relationship you'd like to change. Ask him or her to describe how it could be different.
4. Look through a magazine and cut out pictures of what you'd like the change to look like.
5. Ask your inner child what he or she needs and wants. Use that information to create a picture of change.

Step 3: Identify your stumbling blocks

Step 3 makes you look at what you might do consciously or unconsciously to sabotage your plan. This includes complaining and whining about change or making problems for yourself that you don't have. We've included many of these stumbling blocks each week of your therapy in the **Obstacles to Growth and Change** sections to alert you to some common ways you might prevent yourself from moving forward. When you're aware of these in advance, you're less likely to get off track.

Step 4: Plan a rehearsal

Now that you have a plan, it's time to try it out in safety. You get to do a trial run. Pretend the situation is at hand. Get some friends to take on the other parts. Practice the behaviors you planned. How did it go for you, for the others? How are you feeling? How are the others feeling? Do you want to make any adjustments? Practice it again with the changes. Check things out again.

Step 5: Follow through with action

This is when you actually do what you have planned. There is no substitute for action. Taking action allows you to be proactive, instead of reacting to situations. It will enable you to make real the changes

---

(!) Hint   Common stumbling blocks

1. Beware of using the word "try." It's better not to predict failure or set up an excuse in advance. Either do something or don't.
2. Picture eating a Thanksgiving turkey in one bite. Unrealistic? You bet. Making changes is unrealistic if you are attempting to do everything at once. Break down the change you want to accomplish into small, manageable pieces and be realistic in your expectations. Do one thing at a time.
3. This bears repeating. If you are comparing yourself to someone else, you will stop yourself from making changes or enjoying the process.

that you want in your life. The more you practice in the real world, the better you get. Don't be surprised if others don't jump up and applaud at the first signs of change. The changes you make may be threatening to them. Keep focused on your plan.

If you feel uncertain, adopt an attitude of confidence. Act as if you can already do what you intend. Twelve-step programs call this step "Fake it till you make it." With such an attitude, you can do what you never dreamed was possible, instead of stopping yourself before you start.

Step 6: Reevaluate your plan

Look back and see how your plan worked. Are you satisfied with the results? Do you want to continue with your plan? Do you need to make any changes or adjustments? This is the time for fine-tuning and encouraging yourself to keep going. Make a date with yourself in another week to check in and keep tabs on your progress. You can always make an adjustment or alter the plan—it's not etched in stone. Knowing you can change your mind and make modifications will help you take the steps.

Carmen's story

Carmen found that she had gained a few pounds each year for the past 10 years and now was horrified when she stepped on her scale. She hadn't been happy with how she looked for some time. Now that she was approaching her 50th birthday, it was time to do something. In the past, she'd talked about going on a diet, but after a few days of denying herself the foods she loved, she had given up in disgust. She was ready to make a change. Using our six-step outline, Carmen developed her action plan.

First, she created a picture by asking a friend who attended Weight Watchers to tell her what a healthy weight range was for her height. From that information, she set a goal weight for herself. Then, she found a picture of herself at that weight and stuck it on her bathroom mirror. She planned her steps by deciding to join Weight Watchers, choosing a meeting she could attend once a week for 10 weeks, walking for 30 minutes three times a week, and going to bed earlier on the nights before her walks.

Next, Carmen identified her stumbling blocks she might use to sabotage herself. They included not going to meetings, going to bed late so she was too tired to get up, hitting the snooze button, turning over and going back to sleep if it was raining, believing her son would starve if she didn't make his breakfast, and thinking that if she didn't lose a lot of weight right away, her plan was stupid and she should give it up. She realized she had plenty of ways to stop herself, but she was ready to take the next step and planned a rehearsal.

Carmen's biggest worry was how to get out the door in the morning without having to wait on her son. She asked a friend to help her rehearse what she would do. Her friend played the part of Carmen's son, doing everything he might think of to keep her busy with him. By accident, Carmen discovered while rehearsing with her friend, that when she smiled at her "son" and said, "I know you can handle this," and continued on, her "son" was at a loss and gave up trying to stop her from going for her walk.

She was ready to follow through with action. On her first morning, when the alarm rang, she opened one eye and reached for the snooze button. Instead of hitting it, she gave herself a pep talk and got out of bed. She had her exercise clothes out and jumped into them. After she was dressed, she kissed her son, walked out the door, hopped in the car, put a note on her steering wheel to remind her of her Thursday meeting, and drove to the park to walk. She didn't analyze or question; she just put one foot in front of the other and followed her plan.

At the end of the first week, Carmen reevaluated her plan. She noticed that her son had skipped breakfast three mornings, so she decided to make extra waffles on Sunday so he could pop them in the toaster when she went for her walk. She called a friend who liked to walk and invited her to join her in the mornings. She was delighted when her friend said yes. Carmen knew that if she was meeting someone, she'd give herself that extra push to get out of bed in the mornings. At her first Weight Watchers meeting, she found she'd only lost one pound. Instead of focusing on the number of pounds, she decided to acknowledge that she was losing weight, and she felt encouraged. After continuing with her plan for the next two months, Carmen was close to meeting her goal. Taking action had made the difference.

With action there are no secrets. Once you decide to do something, you'll either do it or you won't. If you do it, you will experience change; if you don't, nothing is likely to improve. Your action will always show your real intentions. We call this "speaking with two tongues." (Once again, we give thanks to Steve Cunningham for his creativity and insight.) The tongue in your mouth stands for your words and the tongue in your shoe for your actions. With which tongue do you speak? When you do what you say, you'll feel better and have a richer quality of life. When you change your actions, your feelings and your thoughts shift in turn.

Creating changes in your world

Understanding the connection between thinking, feeling, and doing can put you in the driver's seat of your life. With this information, you can recognize where difficulties occur. Then you can decide which path—whether it's thinking, feeling, or doing—to follow when you're making changes. Look at the **Obstacles for Growth and Change** and identify what might stop you from moving forward; use one of the suggestions from the list of **Easy Steps for Change** each day. The **Activities** section provides exercises to help you practice making changes in your thinking, feeling, and actions.

Obstacles to growth and change

See if any of the following are ways that you stop yourself from making changes.

1. If you'd rather not invest the time and energy to understand your thinking, you'll continue to react automatically and continue your mischief.
2. If you continue to think others see the world the same way that you do, you'll be unable to make room for differences.
3. Thinking in absolutes like "always" and "never" will shrink your options and stunt your growth.
4. Believing that you could never change, thinking that your old patterns are your only options, is sure to keep you stuck.
5. Not paying attention to the warning lights on your "dashboard" of feelings could lead you to blowing up or burning out.
6. Judging or limiting feelings can make you sick.
7. Thinking your feelings instead of feeling them will prevent you from building intimacy in relationships.
8. You may be making the common mistake of taking other people's anger at you personally, instead of realizing that their anger is information about them.

9. If you think you must have a good reason to be angry, you're not likely to recognize the feeling when it comes up. You may tend to store up many small, unexpressed grievances until you explode in a dramatic (and possibly dangerous) display of what you perceive as righteous anger.

10. If you don't follow through with action on what you say you'll do, change will be illusive.

11. If you believe that everyone shows and feels love in the same way, you'll probably find you're missing out on feeling loved, and feel unappreciated for your efforts to show love.

12. If you think you have to win another person over to your way of thinking, you'll be so busy making your case that you'll waste everyone's time instead of getting to what you want.

13. If you believe that your ideas aren't important, or are afraid voicing them will make a situation worse, you may hold back and keep your opinions to yourself. Then, no one will know what you think or feel, and can't jump in to help.

14. Staying closed to alternative approaches to healing may keep you sick.

Easy steps for change

Change is rarely easy, but if you follow the suggestions below you'll be on your way.

- ☑ If it's on your mind, put it on your lips.
- ☑ Make sure that the tongue in your mouth matches the tongue in your shoe.
- ☑ Pay attention to your feelings. Make a list, writing one feeling you have each day. Use the feeling faces on page 169 to help you identify and name them.
- ☑ Share one feeling out loud with someone each day.
- ☑ Don't get caught in magical thinking; trust others to be who they are instead of who you want them to be. Remember that a poisonous snake is still a poisonous snake, even if it's curled up asleep in a ball.
- ☑ Check out what others are thinking instead of making assumptions. Work towards getting matching pictures.
- ☑ Allow for style differences and separate realities. It's amazing we ever see anything the same way someone else does.

☑ You can want anything you want and ask for it, but that doesn't mean you'll get it.

☑ Decide what you will do to get your needs met.

☑ Use an "I feel...because..." message to share your thinking and feelings and to invite more genuine listening and less defensiveness from others.

☑ To avoid unsafe or disrespectful displays, learn to recognize the physical manifestations of anger in your body, and teach yourself to calm down before confronting people.

☑ If you're frightened or put off by the way someone else expresses anger, let him or her know that you're willing to hear about the feelings, but you're unwilling to be abused. Say that if that happens, you'll remove yourself until he or she is calmer and can speak respectfully, then do it.

☑ Make an action plan for one thing you could do this week to improve a relationship.

☑ Get a massage.

☑ Draw a picture of a feeling you have and share it with a friend.

☑ While talking to a friend, put your hand on your head, your heart, and your gut and see what happens.

☑ Ask someone if the way you show love helps them feel loved. Ask if there's something else they'd like.

☑ Write an anger letter to someone you're feeling anger towards and talk about your feeling. You don't need to send it—you may tear the letter up, put it in a drawer, or send it. However, if you want to send it, reread it a day or two after writing it, before putting it in the mail.

☑ Give yourself permission to listen to your feelings and trust them to guide you.

 ## Activities

1. Here's a way to get in touch with separate realities. Write out your answers to the following:

   ☑ What relationship would you like to work on?
   ☑ What are your thoughts about this relationship?
   ☑ What do you think the other person's thoughts are?

   You may not have noticed or paid attention, but think about how you're feeling when you picture this relationship and write down your feelings. Don't forget to look at the feeling faces on page 169 for help. If you listened to your feelings and let them guide you, where would they take you? What would you do?

2. If you haven't already done this exercise do it here. Think of a situation you want to change. Write a feeling you have about it in the center circle below. Then write what you do when you have that feeling in the last circle. Decide what you are thinking (what's that voice in your head saying?) and write that in the first circle. Think about what your goal is. Does your current pattern get you to your goal? If not, create a new pattern in the second set of circles that will take you to your goal.

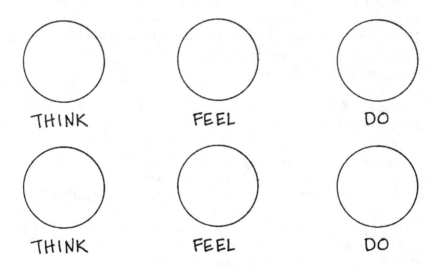

THINK　　　　FEEL　　　　DO

THINK　　　　FEEL　　　　DO

3. To increase your awareness of feelings, write the answers to the following questions:
   - ☑ What am I feeling?
   - ☑ Where did it come from?
   - ☑ How does it serve me?
   - ☑ How long do I want to keep it (minutes, hours, days)?
   - ☑ What will I put in its place?

4. This exercise will help you learn how your feelings help you or stop you from achieving your goals. (Thanks to Lynn Lott, Marilyn Kentz, and Dru West for letting us reprint these activities from their book *To Know Me Is to Love Me.*) Start by listing three feelings you had today. Next to them write

how you would prefer to feel. When you feel the way you did, what do you usually do? If you practice those behaviors, do you end up with the feelings you'd like to have? If not, what other actions could you take? Consider these options:

☑ Talking with someone else, asking for ideas.

☑ Sharing your feelings with a friend.

☑ Pretending you have a magic wand and making changes.

☑ Thinking of the advice you'd give to a friend who wanted to make these changes and giving the advice to yourself.

5. Think of something you're angry about. What is it? To deal with anger, it helps to know at whom or what it is directed. Is it at yourself? At someone else? At someone else's anger at you? At life? At an absent other (someone who has died, moved away, become chemically dependent, or emotionally unavailable)? Every person who is feeling angry has some underlying issue. To find yours, you'll need to keep asking yourself, "What about that makes me angry...and what about *that* makes me angry...?" until you're getting the same answer over and over. Are your underlying issues about recognition (what people think about you), power (wanting your way), justice (fairness), or skills (being good enough)? Go back to Week 6 for ideas on what to do for yourself to make changes in your behavior based on what underlying issues you discover. (This exercise was adapted from the work of Mitch Messer.)

6. Laughter is good for all of us. Laugh often so you don't take yourself (and life) too seriously. How many times have you laughed today? At what? When was the last time you laughed at yourself? Who makes you laugh? Whom do you make laugh?

7. Of all the earth's creatures only humans can cry. Can you remember the last time you cried? What feelings did you have? What was going on? Is there something happening in your current life that you need to cry about?

8. Write out a recent dream. What is the feeling you have from it? What is a current life problem that you are dealing with? How could that feeling help you stay stuck? How could you use that feeling to help you improve your situation? How could it help you make things worse?

9. Ask for love in a way that you feel most loved, remembering that others aren't mind readers. They need to learn what helps you feel loved.

 **Week 8**

Keep Your Change Healthy

D
o you think all your problems are your fault? Or do you think that you have a mental illness or a genetic defect? Are you waiting for someone else to shape up, behave, or get some help so your life will be better? Maybe you believe you are just unlucky. This week's therapy involves learning to think about problems in a new way.

We believe that all human problems involve relating to others. A person's mental, emotional, and physical health, and well-being are influenced by the amount of what Alfred Adler called "gemeinschaftsgefuehl." Gemeinschaftsgefuehl (usually translated as "social interest") refers to a person's feeling of community, or sense of connection to a group (a marriage, a family, an office, and so forth). Adler taught that you would feel and act better if you worked on improving the social interest in all your relationships. This means connecting and contributing, while practicing mutual respect—respect for yourself and others. It means emphasizing *cooperation* rather than *competition* in all of your relationships. It also means recognizing that all humans have equal value in spite of their differences.

This week, you will see how any problem you have involves all the players in a relationship. Each has a different picture or part of what is going on. Instead of blaming yourself, blaming others, or feeling victimized by circumstances, you will find out how to feel and act better by replacing unhealthy relationships with relationships that are respectful, cooperative, and horizontal. You can use these techniques to work on improving relationships with friends, family, people at work, romantic partners, children, peers, and even with yourself.

What is a relationship?

We find that most people don't have a clear picture of what a relationship is. Well, we would like to introduce you to the good boat *S.S. Relation Ship.* (See the diagrams below.) We find that it helps to think of a difficult situation by visualizing it as a ship with all the people who are part of the problem on board, relating. Here are some different ways the relation-ship might look.

Notice that in this ship, one person is rowing forward, while the other rows backward—the ship is going nowhere. Marion drew this "relation-ship" with Patrick, illustrating her view of their opposing approaches to parenting. Her goal was to raise obedient children who respected their elders, asking, "How high, ma'am?" when she told them to jump. Patrick's approach, on the other hand, could be summed up as "Question authority." She realized that the problem was that they often contradicted each other's decisions about their children's expected and allowed behavior when they disciplined them.

Toby recently opened a restaurant with a partner. In this picture of their relationship, he drew himself doing all the rowing, while his partner napped. He immediately understood why he was so resentful and could see that he was feeling overwhelmed and undersupported as he shouldered the bulk of the responsibility for the fate of the business.

Susan felt lonely and left behind since her bosom buddy Annie had married and become pregnant. All Annie talked about was medical insurance, mortgages, and establishing a new family with her husband. Their time together had grown limited, and Susan worried that by still leading "the single life" and working for the same orthodontist for 10 years, she had little to contribute to the excitement her friend was feeling whenever they were together. Susan drew herself being dragged and holding on to a flimsy line behind the ship rowed by Annie.

Gerry thinks he is following the values his father taught him: working hard, saving money, keeping physically and socially active, and so forth. Yet, he's unhappy, bored, and dissatisfied. When he visits his parents, they quiz him about the details of his life and then his father proceeds to offer all kinds of directives to improve his life. He thinks Gerry should be more accepting of how life is and not expecting everything to be perfect. Gerry's ship shows his father in the stern with a megaphone in hand criticizing his every stroke as Gerry rows furiously.

Consider the relationship you want to work on this week and think about what your relationship would look like. Take a few minutes to draw a relation-ship before continuing on with the chapter, so you will have an image to refer back to as you identify ways to improve it.

Is your relationship healthy or unhealthy?

As you look at the previous diagrams or at the one you just drew, imagine that you are telling a friend what to look for in a good relation-ship. This could be a relationship in the workplace, in a friendship, or with an intimate partner. Would you tell your friend to look for rela-tionships like the ones pictured? Would you tell him or her to look for someone who is critical, withdrawn, dictatorial, mean-spirited, under-mining, dishonest, or mocking? Of course you wouldn't! However, you may be putting up with a lot because you don't believe the relationship can be different, or because you don't know how to go about changing it. You may feel discouraged and powerless to make a difference.

If you are like a lot of people, you might not realize that your rela-tionships aren't healthy, because you may not have had much experi-ence with healthy relationships. Here's a list to help you recognize "healthy" when you see it. Look carefully at which of the healthy quali-ties you have in your relationship. Which qualities are missing? No rela-tionship is 100-percent healthy or unhealthy, but usually lies somewhere on a continuum between the two.

In addition to helping you assess the health of your current relation-ships, this list can guide you to where you want to go and what you might want to work on. If you looked at the list and noticed that the relationship troubling you has very few of the healthy qualities, don't despair. If you really want to improve it, you need to believe the small steps you take can make big ripples. In this chapter, you will find many ways to take these small steps to create and maintain healthier relationships.

Look at the two circles on page 192. The more you use and practice the ideas in this chapter, the more you will be able to move from Circle A to Circle B. Although they appear to be the same, there is a big differ-ence: Circle A represents an unhealthy relationship, while Circle B is a healthy one.

The difference is this: An unhealthy relationship is one in which you feel terrible most of the time, but for a brief time you practice some of the healthy qualities in the list. A healthy relationship is just the opposite. When you are operating in that small section of the pie where

things don't feel good to you, both of you are working to get your relationship back on track. Sometimes people think they have a good relationship
when things are going well for a small amount of time. They deceive themselves by thinking they have to settle for just a small slice of the good stuff.

! Hint   Qualities of a healthy relationship

☑ Respect others and yourself.
☑ Feel safe, trusting others.
☑ Be yourself and be appreciated for who you are.
☑ Have fun together.
☑ Have time to yourself.
☑ Practice cooperation, instead of competition.
☑ Look forward to mutual growth.
☑ Share common interests.
☑ Encourage relationships outside the primary relationship.
☑ Practice give and take.
☑ Use win/win conflict-resolution methods.
☑ Communicate honestly.
☑ Share and listen to another's feelings without adopting
   them for yourself.
☑ Value differences.
☑ Be curious instead of judgmental.
☑ Let yourself be a learner.
☑ Ask for what you want and need, not expecting others to
   read your mind.
☑ Don't tolerate or give out abuse.

Gwen's story

Gwen thought she had a pretty good relationship before she found out that her partner of 23 years was having an affair with another woman. Gwen and Francesca, had purchased a home together and enjoyed a life of shared interests, passion, and companionship. They never fought and rarely even disagreed about things. Gwen could not understand how this could happen. As the story unfolded, she discovered that Francesca had been secretly involved in this affair for more than a year. When Gwen drew her relationship, she drew Francesca in dotted lines to illustrate that the relationship was an illusion and that Francesca was already on another ship with an unseen person.

As Gwen studied the list of qualities of a healthy relationship and sketched the pie of their recent life together, she recognized that although she and Francesca didn't have any conflicts, they shared only the smallest sliver of the good stuff anymore. She believed it was enough that they bowled together once a week and didn't fight over money. Now she found herself wondering who this person was with whom she had lived for so long, and whether Francesca had any way of knowing what Gwen was really like.

Gwen suspected that if she and Francesca had practiced more of what was on "The Qualities of a Healthy Relationship" list, no third person could have slipped unnoticed between them. If they shared their feelings, asked for what they wanted, spent time with others, and communicated honestly, they might still be together. For Gwen and Francesca it was too late to make improvements, because neither was willing to continue living together under the circumstances. While reading this chapter, if you find one of your relationships lacking in healthy qualities, you don't have to give up on the relationship.

Four paths to healthier relationships

Picture yourself at a crossroad with a sign pointing in four different directions. If you walk down any of these four trails, you will improve your relationships. Or you can pick and choose from each path to help you create the relationships you want and improve the quality of your life. The more you understand and establish aspects from each of these four choices, the quicker you will shift from unhealthy relationships to healthier ones.

Look at where the signs lead. The first sign says, "Take the vertical out of relationships." The second announces, "Become a member of the Encouragement Hall of Fame." Sign number three states, "Replace competition with cooperation." The last reads, "Practice mutually respectful communication." You can start with any of the four paths to enhance your relationships.

Walking down these paths helps you understand why some of your relationships are so uncomfortable and unrewarding. You may have never thought of it this way, but relationships can be either vertical or horizontal. Relationships where you experience the most difficulty and the least satisfaction are more vertical than horizontal.

Taking the vertical out of relationships

In a horizontal relationship, people treat each other as equals, even though they may have differences. Picture a dollar bill and four quarters. Though they have the same value, the paper money is easier to carry in your wallet, while the quarters are more useful if you want to make change or use a coin-operated machine. Horizontal relationships work in much the same way. The people in horizontal relationships have equal value even though they may have different jobs, roles, skills, experiences, and interests in life.

By contrast, in vertical relationships, people do not treat each other as though they have equal importance. In subtle and often in not so subtle ways, messages are exchanged which say that one person is superior, while the other is inferior. The chart on page 195 gives you more examples of how this works.

Carson's story

Carson, a nurse in a family physician's office for 10 years, knew many of the patients well. Part of Carson's job was to give injections to

Horizontal vs. vertical relationships

To have horizontal relationships:	To have vertical relationships:
Treat others as equals.	Treat others as either inferior or superior.
Encourage others and promote self-confidence.	Discourage others and promote feelings of inadequacy.
Stimulate positive feelings.	Stimulate negative feelings.
Solicit disclosure, discussions, alternatives, contribution, and openness.	Insist your way is the right way.
Love yourself and treat others well.	Put yourself down and criticize, correct, punish, and threaten others.
Promote equality.	See yourself or others as a "just a..." (just a trainee, just a victim, just a woman, and so forth).
Practice give and take.	Expect others to take care of you, and think of yourself as entitled.
Work to create win/win solutions.	Boss, obey, or look for blame.
Be firm and kind.	Be permissive or autocratic.
Emphasize cooperation.	Emphasize competition and power over others.
Rely on the power of love.	Have a love of power.
Value differences.	Insist on the "right" and "wrong" ways of doing things.
Practice mutual respect.	Practice moral superiority.
Make room for everyone to learn.	Confer the status of "expert" on a few.
Think in terms of "ours."	Think in terms of "mine, "yours," or "theirs."
Have an attitude of curiosity.	Have a know-it-all attitude.
Take responsibility for your own behavior and expect others to do the same.	Blame, judge, criticize, and look for fault.
Change yourself.	Try to change or control others.
Practice emotional honesty.	Use displays of emotion to intimidate and manipulate others.

adults and children, tetanus boosters to injured workers, and vaccinations to overseas travelers. He had learned over the years that even the most sophisticated patient could be a baby when it came to needles. Carson was skilled at painless injections and practiced at putting even the most frightened patient at ease. With genuine interest, he quizzed patients about their lives, and as they chatted away about themselves, he went about the task of "sticking" them. His patients liked him and appreciated his skill.

Once a patient who was a pilot invited Carson to have coffee. Carson declined, concerned he would have nothing to say about himself, even though he would have liked to learn more about the pilot's experiences. As social as he appeared with his patients, at office parties Carson kept to himself. He didn't feel he fit in with the other nurses, who were female, and he also felt uneasy joining the conversation of the doctors and their spouses, whom he thought of as more "worldly" than he.

One day, a busy tax accountant verbally attacked him, and shouted complaints to the receptionist because Carson had accidentally injected him with the wrong medicine. Even though Carson apologized and explained that the drug would not harm him, the patient was furious because he had to come back the next day to check on the effects of the first injection.

Even though the rest of the office staff reassured Carson that there was not a nurse alive who had not either mixed up a drug or given a wrong dose of a medication, Carson found himself dreading work. He felt shaky and nauseous every time he readied a shot, afraid he would injure a patient. As the weeks went on Carson was constantly on edge.

It wasn't until he read an article about vertical and horizontal relationships that Carson realized his discomfort at office social functions and his daily anxiety over injecting certain patients were related. Scanning the columns, he could see that he had put himself in vertical relationships with the accountant and the office staff. The excitable accountant who had intimidated Carson with his display of anger treated Carson as his inferior. He made Carson feel inadequate by criticizing and threatening him. Carson, who regarded the man as above him, saw himself as "just" a nurse and the accountant as an "expert." He believed the customer was always right. Although Carson thought the accountant was an unreasonable jerk, he still put himself down for his mistake and blamed himself for not being able to control the patient's reaction.

Socially, when the office got together at the holidays or for training, Carson kept to himself because he saw the doctors as above him and the physician assistants and bookkeepers as below him. By the same token, he could never have a conversation over coffee with a pilot if he had already decided that he could never measure up.

Carson studied the horizontal side of the chart and was relieved to find that he was also doing many things that invited less vertical relationships. He was good at encouraging patients (especially children) and kept them calm when they felt nervous. He stimulated positive feelings and a sense of security in most of his patients and treated others well. He was already taking responsibility for his own behavior and working on changing himself.

Carson decided he would work on creating more behaviors on the horizontal side of the chart and minimizing those from the vertical side. He realized he could use his natural curiosity to create less stuffy relationships with the office staff. The next time the office had a get-together, Carson made a point of talking with one of the doctors, asking him questions about practicing medicine. He asked one of the receptionists what her tricks were for dealing with obnoxious people on the phone without losing them as patients. And the next time he approached a nervous "big shot" patient, needle in hand, Carson disclosed, "You probably wouldn't believe me if I told you, this is probably more uncomfortable for me than it is for you."

Carson noticed that he no longer hated going to work or felt sick when he gave injections to the patients. As he walked the path marked "Take the vertical out of relationships," he experienced better relationships and more joy in his life.

Problems caused by competition

Many people grew up in families where their parents' vertical relationship and family values created an atmosphere of competition, so they never learned what a cooperative and horizontal relationship looks like. When you work on minimizing competition and maximizing cooperation, you can enjoy your relationships more.

You may not have thought of competition as comparing yourself to others vertically. But when you compare yourself to someone else, you usually end up feeling like a "winner" or a "loser" based on the absolute judgments you started developing as a little kid. This is not the same as noticing how you differ from others. It is not the same as realizing that others may have a lot to offer that can help you learn to do things differently. Rather, we are referring to comparisons that make you feel not good enough.

When you were young, competition may have played a big part in how you were parented. Your parents said things like, "Don't act like your brother," or "Why can't you be a good little girl like your sister?" You may have grown up in an area where you were considered better than someone else if you were the "right" religion, color, or economic status. You may have been compared or compared yourself to other children vertically in terms of your talents, abilities, efforts, and accomplishments. This is common especially in school, where letter grades show you how you measure up against others. Remember the star charts for good behavior or books read, or the black checks next to your name if you misbehaved? These told you at a glance where you stood in relation to others.

These are all forms of competition that focus on "self-interest." They all take away your ability to feel capable, connected, and cared for—all important parts of your social interest. Being on a vertical ladder with others is precarious, whether you are above them or below them.

Even being "one up" on others can be discouraging. When you are above, you have to work to maintain your position, making sure no one catches up, passes you, or pulls you down. Being "above," you are dependent on having someone "below." It's difficult to increase your social interest when you have decided you are either better or worse than others—tracking which rung of the ladder you are on takes so much energy and attention.

There is very little energy left over to do what needs to be done to meet the needs of the situation. "Meeting the needs of the situation" is how we refer to acting out of a sense of community feeling or social interest instead of acting out of self-interest.

Comparing yourself to others is something you did as a child to understand who you were. Now that you are grown, you have the ability to see that because a family member, colleague, spouse, or friend might be really good at something, doesn't mean you cannot strive to master

Hint   Cooperation is not blind obedience

The word *cooperation* is often used when what is really meant is, "do what I say." However, we see cooperation as people working together, like the four wheels on a wagon. Cooperation is when two people help each other lift or move a heavy object.

Cooperation is also different from compromise, where everyone has to give up something and lose something. In cooperative relationships, the search is for win/win agreements where everyone feels as if his or her needs are being met. To find win/win solutions, it is important for people to learn the language of mutually respectful communication.

the same skill in your own way. You also learn that you do not have to be as good or better than others for your contribution to count.

Working to create more cooperation and less competition in your relationships will not only help *you* feel better and do better, but others in the relationship will feel better as well. If you have children, they will benefit too. In today's society, we have a long way to go before we get past the negative effects of competition. Instead, we must learn to value differences and diversity. We have to learn to work together toward common goals, instead of keeping score on who is better than whom.

Bill and Christy's story

Bill and Christy struggled with competition in their relationship, though on the surface it looked like something else. Christy frequently stopped Bill in midsentence in front of her parents when personal issues, such as therapy, were mentioned. In her family, talking about such personal matters in public was "airing dirty laundry." In Bill's family, on the other hand, she noticed everyone had his or her nose in everybody else's business, to the point where she could hardly stand to be with them. His sisters were constantly trying to "fix" her, and his mother and father seemed to expect her to tell them her deepest secrets. Neither Bill nor Christy thought this interaction was competitive—they categorized it as a privacy issue.

As embarrassed as Christy was by Bill's disclosures to her parents, Bill was equally upset when she cut him off. After sharing some of the ideas in *Do-It-Yourself Therapy*, they had a frank discussion about their interactions. Bill revealed that he felt hurt and judged when she interrupted him. It occurred to Christy that as she compared her family to Bill's, she was feeling "one up," mentally putting him down, because she thought what he and his family did was wrong. "That's why I feel put down," Bill countered. "You act like your way is better. It hurts. I wish that you'd accept that we just do it differently."

"I try, but you are just like my brother," Christy said. "He always caught on to everything so quickly. In school the teachers would say, 'Oh, you're Bobby's sister; we hope you do as well as he did!' But I didn't. The fact is, I hated school. I had a hard time. I was in the lowest reading group and I got in a lot of trouble. I didn't go to college because I figured I would never do as well as everyone else. And on top of it, you remind my parents of my brother, and I think when you talk about us, you look like 'Mr. Brilliant' and they take your side. It makes me want to give up, like I did in school."

Christy had tears in her eyes as she finished talking. Bill leaned over and put his arm around her, saying gently, "There's more to this than airing dirty laundry and maintaining privacy. Christy, you don't have to compete with Bobby or with me. Let's put our heads together and think of something that will work for both of us."

"Okay," Christy replied, "I'm willing, but I'm still uncomfortable. I still need more privacy for myself, even if you don't."

"I'll make you a deal," Bill said. "Let's try for an agreement. Let's work on this until we come up with a plan we both feel good about. I'll stop talking to my family about our therapy, as long as I know that we'll keep the conversation open until we both feel comfortable with a plan." Christy nodded in agreement and both of them heaved a sigh of relief. The notion of a win/win solution was a novel concept to two people who thought the only way to get along was to fight.

Mutually respectful communication

When the people who are part of a problem talk openly and honestly with each other, things can only get better. As you may recall from Week 3, mutual respect is the art of respecting the self, as well as others. Not only does mutual respect permeate healthy relationships, it also has a language of its own. This language is the fourth path for creating and maintaining healthy relationships. As you follow this path, you might think of yourself as a "social" pioneer. You are practicing ways to motivate others to discover win/win solutions, use group problem-solving, practice firmness and kindness to empower (not overpower) others, and communicate respectfully.

Marjorie's story

By being direct, taking others seriously, and valuing their differences, Marjorie was able to change the environment at work to one that was more cooperative and less competitive. This was not normally the case. Although different groups in the agency were supposed to work together to help clients, people in each group did their own thing instead of following through with what they had agreed upon. People felt angry about this "sneaky" behavior, complaining to their colleagues about how difficult the other people were to work with, instead of speaking face to face. There was very little trust or respect between the groups.

Marjorie decided to ask directly for what she wanted, speaking up about what was working and what wasn't. She asked others what they thought instead of talking behind their backs, and found that her trust level was improving. Marjorie could say, "I don't think what you are recommending will work for me, but I'd like to try to understand your thinking before I make my decision. Maybe we're not as far apart as I think."

Respectful communication at work and home

When everyone is allowed to contribute and participate in decision-making, they feel empowered rather than overcontrolled. One of the best ways to create this environment at work is to hold regularly scheduled staff meetings. These are not meetings held when there is a crisis or when the boss arbitrarily decides it's time to have one. Start the regularly scheduled meeting with compliments, appreciation, and acknowledgments. Ask everyone at the meeting what he or she would like to put on the agenda, or use an agenda book (or box) in which people can write in between meetings to create an agenda. After giving compliments and writing the agenda on a flip chart or board that all can see, prioritize the agenda with the group members, as well as setting up time limits for each item on the agenda. Then ask for someone to volunteer to be a timekeeper. If the timer goes off before an item is completed, poll group members to find out if they would like to give more time to the issue and save other items for a later meeting, or if they would prefer to table the item and move on.

Discuss each agenda item (unless the person who put the item on the agenda feels it already has been resolved by the meeting time) without blame or criticism, and work together to brainstorm solutions. Brainstorming means generating as many ideas as possible, quickly, without judgment or evaluation. If an issue is too difficult to resolve at one sitting, hold a discussion to learn what everyone thinks about the issue and table it until the next regularly scheduled meeting for continued discussion. Whenever possible, it is best to achieve a consensus before making changes. If a consensus can't be reached and a decision needs to be made, the manager can say, "We need to do such and such until we can work out an agreement we can all live with. We'll keep communication open and continue our discussions at our meetings until that time."

Family meetings help "get horizontal"

Just as staff meetings go a long way toward making or breaking the morale in a work environment, family meetings can be a place where everyone has a chance to feel they can make a contribution. Family meetings are like social interest labs. The principles are the same as for staff meetings. They should be regularly scheduled, the jobs of chairing and recording should be rotated, an agenda to which anyone may add items during the week should be followed, consensus or temporary interim decisions should be sought. It's very important to include compliments and appreciation, to practice the idea that working together means identifying the positive and not just focusing on problems. (For in-depth material about family meetings and how you can use them to transform the atmosphere in your home, see *Chores Without Wars* by Lynn Lott and Riki Intner or *Positive Discipline A-Z* by Jane Nelsen, Lynn Lott, and H. Stephen Glenn.)

More tips for communicating respectfully

To promote respectful, noncompetitive relationships, it is important to take time to learn and practice our four tips for mutually respectful communication. The quickest way to improve communication is the easiest to do but the hardest to start—to listen instead of talk. The second lesson, practicing emotional honesty, is the process of getting in touch with your thoughts and feelings and having the courage to express them. It also means learning to listen to others without judging, criticizing, or defending. Using encouraging language, the third tip, means learning how to give and receive compliments and appreciation, instead of praise and criticism. The final lesson, "less is more," uses techniques that invite dialogue and closeness, including communicating in sentences of 10 words or less, using just one word or a signal, or writing a note instead of conversing face-to-face.

Victoria's story

Victoria grew up poor in Florida, assisting her father at his seaside souvenir stand after school, weekends, and summers. As a little girl, she watched the happy, wealthy tourists, and unconsciously made a decision that people like her were not as good as those people who had money.

Now, as an adult and married to a dentist, she lives a middle-class life in a middle-class neighborhood. Her daughter is friends with children whose parents are doctors, lawyers, and successful businesspeople. Her childhood decision that she was "less than" makes it hard for Victoria to feel comfortable around the neighborhood children and their parents. She is always a little uneasy, afraid that she is not as smart as the other parents, that she is bound to say something stupid sooner or later, that the others have more social graces.

When Victoria was introduced to the four tips for mutually re-spectful communication at a PTA program, she thought this might help her make some friends because she felt isolated and lonely. Victoria decided to take some risks by putting herself in situations she had been avoiding. When Maryann and Martha invited her to help bake cupcakes for the Halloween carnival, she made the leap. (By the way, Lynn, Riki, and Barbara are available to speak at your PTA. For infor-mation, call 707-526-3141 or 797-769-9631.)

Victoria starts with "just listen"

Victoria figured that she would try the easiest tip first. As Maryann and Martha chatted away about their children, the teachers, school poli-tics, and their marriages, Victoria was quiet but interested. To her sur-prise, the women expressed many of the same opinions she held but had never stated openly for fear of looking stupid. It was amazing how much Victoria felt involved in the conversation simply by keeping her lips to-gether, nodding and saying only, "Mmmmm. Ooooh. Unhuh. Uhuh."

Victoria uses emotional honesty

Victoria discovered that when people felt listened to, they were also interested in hearing what she had to say. When Maryann asked her what she thought about the school's decision to give up trick-or-treating and have a carnival instead, Victoria felt uncomfortable, but she took a deep breath, and trying out the formula from the handout she got at the PTA function, she said, "I feel a little nervous because I'm a shy person."

Martha jumped in, saying, "Well, we thought you didn't like us because you are always so quiet and you would rush out of meetings before we even got a chance to say hello."

"I'm sorry that I gave that impression. I have been feeling very iso-lated and could use some friends. Today has been special for me and I hope we can do more things together in the future. I wonder if you would come by for coffee someday while our children are playing after school."

Victoria practices encouraging language

Victoria found it easy to extend appreciation and compliments to Martha and Maryann, even though when she was growing up and work-ing for her father, she was used to hearing praise or criticism. If her father liked what she was doing, he would tell her she was a "good girl," but when he was angry, he would say things like, "Can't you get anything right? Never leave money lying on the counter while you are making change! Where is your brain?"

Victoria told Martha that she liked how outspoken she was and wished she could be more like her. Martha blushed and said, "I'm always opening my mouth and shoving my foot in all the way up to my knee." "Oh, no," Victoria said, "You say what you think and that helps me feel more comfortable because I don't have to wonder how you feel."

Victoria learns that "less is more"

Although she was very quiet and shy in social situations, Victoria was the opposite at home, going on and on about what she wanted from both her husband and her daughter. The two of them would nod their heads in agreement, but both were "deaf" to her words. This would be a perfect place to try out the "less is more" method.

The first option, "communicate in 10 words or less," was a snap and it immediately wiped the blank stare from her husband's face that Victoria was so used to seeing. When Victoria took her husband's hand and said simply, "The garage is a mess. Help me clean it," (only nine words) her husband actually stood up and headed for the garage.

When the phone rang and he was sidetracked, Victoria waited until he was done with his call, looked him in the eye, and tried the second variation, using just use one word. She only had to say "garage," and he said, "oh yeah," and made for the door once again. Victoria was in shock.

She decided to use a note with her daughter instead of repeating herself over and over without any positive results. When her daughter put her key in the front door after school, she couldn't help but notice the note pinned to the door:

Victoria watched as her daughter, note, coat, backpack, and shoes in hand, walked to her bedroom.

Gradually, Victoria recognized that the more she practiced mutually respectful communication at school on PTA projects, in the classroom, or with acquaintances in town, people were appreciative. They were glad to see her, and clearly seemed to like her. The

Please take your coat, backpack and shoes to your room. love, mom risks she was willing to take to change were worth the effort, as she felt less lonely and isolated.

Creating changes in your world

Information and awareness can improve a relationship. As the saying goes, "If you don't know where you're going, you might just end up there." Now you know that healthy relationships are about the social interest that comes from mutual respect, cooperation, and horizontal attitudes and behavior. Paying attention to your own behavior or that of others may seem like a lot of work, and at first it is. The path will not be a straight line, but using the principles in this chapter will help you adjust your course and make progress. As you become a student of human nature and acquire more people skills, you will discover options that will help you feel better and operate more effectively.

Look at the following **Obstacles to Growth and Change** to see which are barriers between you and the healthier relationships you would like to have. Select and practice some of the **Easy Steps for Change** this week and do your homework in the real world by trying out one or more of the **Activities** at the end of the chapter.

Obstacles to growth and change

1. You are surrounded by unhealthy relationships. If you assume that what you see on television, in the movies, in the local schools, in many workplaces, and in the families of your friends and relatives is normal (and therefore healthy), then you might be modeling your life and relationships that way. Then you will probably wonder why you feel so miserable and dissatisfied.

2. Our attitude about problems is one of the biggest obstacles you will ever have to tackle. If you think all your problems are your fault, or that there is something wrong with you, you are discouraging yourself and making it harder to make changes. Thinking like this leads to feeling incapable, overwhelmed, permanently flawed, or sick and "unable." From blaming yourself, it's a short step to believing that you don't deserve the greater happiness and satisfaction that come with changing and growing up. If you see yourself as unlucky or a victim of circumstance, there certainly isn't much

you can do about anything. If you are blaming someone else for your difficulties, waiting for someone else to change or behave or get help, you could end up waiting a long time.

3. It is often difficult to recognize unhealthy relationships. You may be so used to settling for a little slice of the good stuff that you have no idea how different your relationship can be. You may be so accustomed to being with a critical, withdrawn, noncommunicative, dictatorial, mean-spirited, indifferent, undermining, dishonest, dismissive, or even abusive partner, that you think this is normal. Do you often go along with what you are *supposed* to do, instead of what you *want* to, thinking that other people know what is best for you? Perhaps you stay stuck because you believe you have not worked hard enough to make the other person change. You may be putting up with unhappy, unhealthy relationships because you don't believe things can be different, or because you don't know how to go about changing them. Maybe you feel powerless to make a difference.

4. If you have the idea that in order to be good enough, a relationship must have all the "healthy" qualities all the time, or that you have to avoid vertical attitudes/behavior in yourself or others all the time, you'll be defeated before you start.

5. If you grew up in a family or community where competition was king, it might take some time to change your thinking and your attitude to a more cooperative/collaborative approach, especially if you are used to being "a winner."

6. Don't expect other people to be thrilled when you decide to change. Chances are that someone will be inconvenienced or upset when you stop following your same old pattern. They will try to get you to return to your "old self," because they will in turn have to take a look at what they do. If you let this scare you out of taking steps, you will find yourself stopped dead in your tracks.

7. If you think listening means correcting, fixing, judging, or defending when someone is sharing their thoughts, feelings, or activities with you, chances are you will short circuit the spirit of cooperation and understanding that can come from mutually respectful communication.

Easy steps for change

☑ If you don't feel good being around some people, limit the amount of time you spend with them.

☑ Increase the amounts of time you spend with people that make you feel good.

☑ Make a list of the qualities that are important to you in a relationship, and take note of how much of that "good stuff" you are getting with each of the important people in your life.

☑ Inventory all of your relationships (family, work, and social) and identify those areas where you are waiting for and expecting someone else to change.

☑ Examine your attitude: Are you blaming yourself or someone else for the problems you have together? Are you thinking you have been unlucky or a victim of circumstance? Try asking yourself, "What choices do I have?" Then decide what you will do.

☑ Practice encouragement in your daily life. Catch yourself being encouraging and make a note of it, either mentally or in your journal.

☑ Create more staff meetings at your place of work.

☑ Institute family meetings at home.

☑ Look for ways to increase cooperation and decrease competition in all your relationships.

☑ Notice when you are comparing yourself to others. Is it encouraging or discouraging you? How?

☑ Pay attention to what you do when you listen to someone else. Are you judging what you are hearing? Trying to fix the problem, giving advice, or rescuing the person? Defending yourself? Criticizing him or her? Try this exercise to say with your body, "I am listening." Keep your lips closed, your eyes on the other person's face, and your head nodding occasionally. If you say anything, it should be a question that clarifies what he or she is telling you.

☑ Try some "less is more" techniques. The next time you have something to say, especially if you've had trouble with talking too much, reduce what you want to get across to just a couple of sentences of 10 words or less. Use a single word or a note if possible.

☑ Practice giving and receiving compliments and appreciation. Appreciation usually sounds like this: "Thank you for," "I appreciate," and so forth. Or describe something someone did that had a positive impact on you: "You make my life easier when you jump in and see what needs doing," "I enjoy your company because you (fill in the blank)," and so forth.

 ## *Activities*

1. What is really important to you in a relationship? Think of a relationship that is troubling you and draw a "relation-ship" with yourself and the other person. What does your picture tell you? Write down your answers to these questions in your journal.

2. Look at the list of qualities of a healthy relationship on page 192 and think of a relationship that is important to you or one that needs improvement. Which qualities are present? Which are missing? Then, look at the two circles on page 192. Picture in your mind the dynamics of the relationship in the last week, or the last month, or the last year. What percentage of the time are you and the other players in the relationship practicing what is on the list of healthy qualities? Does this appear to be a basically healthy relationship, like the circle on the left? Or is it in critical condition, like the one on the right?

3. Think of someone you really dislike being around, or someone with whom you are having difficulties. What qualities does that person possess that invite you to feel irritated, angry, upset, or hopeless? Now look at the chart on page 195. Which column resembles the person you have in mind, or is like the relation-ship the two of you have? Next ask yourself, who is the first person you would call with really good or bad news? Which of the columns in the chart best describes *that* person or relation-ship? Ask yourself how you want others to feel when they are around you. Which of the things on the chart are you willing to do to make that happen? Which do you want to do less of?

4. Examine your family atmosphere and family values (Week 4) for signs of competition. Now think about your current relationships. Where do you see yourself competing and how? Is this competition helpful to you or is it getting in your way? What can you do to change this?

 **Epilogue**

There Is No Finish Line

Congratulations, you have finished your first eight weeks of do-it-yourself therapy. We say "your first eight weeks" because this is only a beginning. We are sure that you will want to continue to grow and change and keep your self-therapy process alive. Hopefully, you will refer back to the information in our book often, as you will learn something new each time you review a section. We'd like our book to become like an old friend with whom you always feel comfortable, or like a favorite walk that feels familiar but different each time you take it. You have the necessary information to create a wonderful quality of life, but it's up to you to make sure you have sufficient practice and exposure to the material so that you will continue to grow.

You may be asking yourself if you are truly a totally new person. In some ways you are—people still recognize you, but by now, you have a different understanding of yourself and of your relationships than before you started your do-it-yourself therapy. You have found new ways of thinking about yourself, others, and life in general. You are experiencing and expressing feelings in new ways and you may be behaving differently. As change takes hold of you, it moves down your body from your head into your heart, into your gut, and finally into your feet. Your thoughts, feelings, and actions all reflect the new you.

Our goal has been to give you information in simple, usable pieces. It may look like we are suggesting change by formula, and in some ways, we do believe that using a formula at first makes an overwhelming process more manageable. As you work with this material, you will notice that this formula gives you a language you can use to communicate about what is happening inside and outside of you, along with a new way to talk about your issues and problems. This could be one more self-help book on your shelf, or it could be like a best friend. What will make the difference is your intention. Notice how Jack, Laura, and Helen put the information together from *Do-It-Yourself Therapy* to create major changes in their lives.

Jack and Laura's story

Although Jack and Laura's marriage was civil and nonabusive, there were too many disappointments and hurt for them to continue. Both decided that a divorce through mediation would be the best option to keep whatever was left in their relationship. Both Jack and Laura had worked with the material in *Do-It-Yourself Therapy* for several years. When it came to the final negotiations in their divorce mediation, they both felt stuck and despite their efforts to keep the process respectful, it was falling apart. On the surface the issue appeared to be about money, but both Jack and Laura knew better they just couldn't identify what their bigger issues were. Laura suggested they review some of the material in the book.

When they reread the material in Week 5, they were able to get unstuck. They each agreed to write out an early childhood memory to look for their deeper issues. Using the methods outlined in the chapter, Jack realized that he wanted the most important woman in his life to acknowledge him, tell him he had done a good job, and assure him that she would be available to comfort him, even after the divorce. He was delaying the process for fear that all their years together were wasted, the break would be all or nothing, and that he would never see Laura again. Laura assured him that he had done a wonderful job supporting the family, that he was important, and that she hoped they would be able to remain friends, helping each other out as needed and even getting together to share meals from time to time.

Laura's issues were different. She was hurt because Jack never asked her what she wanted. When she used a "magic wand" to change her memory, she discovered that she wished Jack would ask her what she wanted and within reason, grant her wishes. Jack had been so busy trying to guess what would be the right thing to do, that it had never occurred to him to ask Laura directly what she wanted. When she told him, he said, "There is nothing you are asking for that I can't give you. Your requests are very reasonable."

Helen's story

Helen, a well-respected financial planner, was working on a business plan that was going nowhere. To improve her work, she went back to early childhood memories to gather information from the past to help her with her present issues. In doing so, she uncovered a memory of planting a garden with her father. It was full of valuable information about what she liked and didn't like, which helped to move her business plan forward.

In the memory, Helen's father told her that her garden could have three rows; he would choose the flowers for two of the rows and she could pick what to put in the last row. He put pansies in one row, Sweet William in another, and she chose gypsophila for the third row. She didn't like the pansies, because they were too disorganized, came in too many colors, and they *always* needed weeding. The Sweet William was fine once the greenery produced fragrant blossoms, but for a little girl of three or four, it was excruciating to wait two years for the plant to bloom. She felt the gypsophila was the best because it was fast growing, very prolific, all one color when it bloomed, manageable, and needing little if no weeding.

Helen realized that the flowers represented the three kinds of clients that she was working with, and currently, she had too many "pansies." Her new business plan would decrease the number of "pansies," those clients who were disorganized, all over the place, and high maintenance, and increase the number of "Sweet Williams." They were the people who didn't pester her, listened to what she said, weren't clingy, had similar opinions on money-management, and didn't blame others.

Last but not least

The title of this book, *Do-It-Yourself Therapy* emphasizes doing your own work. By now you realize that only you can make changes, but we want you to remember that you are part of something bigger than yourself and are never truly alone. That's why we end out our book with an inspirational poem written by a participant who attended a personal growth retreat at author Lynn Lott's Tahoe home.

A tree's growth

Participants were invited to walk into the woods behind Lynn's home to find a tree to commune with. At first, they thought the activity was silly, but they complied nonetheless. Some of the poetry and pictures that have resulted from this activity are truly inspirational, but we believe Celeste Sholl's writing captures perfectly our thoughts about being separate, but not alone. (Thank you Celeste, for your inspirational thoughts and her willingness to share them with others.)

"Trees are like people. I am like you. I could not have grown as big and tall and whole and beautiful if I were in the middle of a clump of trees. I got this big and whole because I have some separateness.

But I am also big and beautiful because I am in the forest in community with my fellow trees. Think of those poor unfortunates who grow alone on a hilltop. The view is great and the sun is warm, but they have no protection from the elements and soon become 'wind trees,' misshapen and stunted with all their branches gone on one side, leaning to try to weather one more storm.

You were meant to be your own person, not to be dependent but interdependent. You will flourish best in the community of other people. Don't stand alone on a hilltop. Be a part of the forest."

Bibliography

Adler, Alfred, *Cooperation Between the Sexes*, New York: Anchor Books, 1978.

Adler, Alfred, *Superiority and Social Interest*, Evanston, IL: Northwestern University Press, 1964.

Adler, Alfred, *What Life Should Mean to You*, New York: Capricorn Books, 1958.

Albert, Linda, *Coping With Kids*, New York: E.P. Dutton, 1982.

Ansbacher, Heinz and Rowena, *The Individual Psychology of Alfred Adler*, New York: Harper Torchbooks, 1964.

Baruth, Leroy and Eckstein, Daniel, *Lifestyle: Theory, Practice, and Research*, Dubuque, IA: Kendall/Hunt Publishing Co., 1978.

Bayard, Robert and Jean, *How to Deal With Your Acting Up Teenager*, San Jose, CA: The Accord Press, 1981.

Bettner, Betty Lou and Lew, Amy, *Raising Kids Who Can*, New York: HarperCollins, 1992.

Christensen, Oscar, *Adlerian Family Counseling*, Minneapolis, MN: Educational Media Corp., 1983.

Corsini, Raymond, *Current Psychotherapies*, Itasca, IL: F.E. Peacock Publishers, 1989.

Corsini, Raymond, *Raising a Responsible Child*, New York: Simon & Schuster, 1978.

Dinkmeyer, Don and Pew, W.L., *Adlerian Counseling and Psychotherapy*, Monterey, CA: Brooks/Cole Publishing, 1979.

Dreikurs, Rudolf, *Psychology in the Classroom*, New York: Harper and Row, 1966.

Dreikurs, Rudolf, *Social Equality: The Challenge of Today*, Chicago: Contemporary Books, Inc., 1971.

Dreikurs, Rudolf, Grunwald, Bernice, and Pepper, Floy, *Maintaining Sanity in the Classroom*, New York: Harper and Row, 1971.

Dreikurs, Rudolf, *Fundamentals of Adlerian Psychology*, Chicago, IL: Adler School of Professional Psychology, 1989.

Dreikurs, Rudolf and Stoltz, V., *Children: The Challenge*, New York: Dutton, 1964.

Faber, Adele and Mazlish, Elaine, *How to Talk So Kids Will Listen and Listen So Kids Will Talk*, New York: Avon, 1982.

Glenn, Stephen H. and Nelsen, Jane, *Raising Self-Reliant Children in a Self-Indulgent World*, Rocklin, CA: Prima Publishing, 1988.

Hay, Louise L., *Heal Your Body*, Carlsbad, CA: Hay House, Inc., 1982, 1984.

Kvols-Riedler, Kathy and Bill, *Understanding Yourself and Others*, Boulder, CO: R.D.I.C. Publications, 1982.

Lott, Lynn and Intner, Riki, *Chores Without Wars*, Rocklin, CA: Prima Publishing, 1998.

Lott, Lynn, Matulich Kentz, Marilyn, and West, Dru, *To Know Me Is to Love Me*, Orem, UT: Empowering People Books, Tapes & Videos, 1990.

Lott, Lynn and West, Dru, *Together and Liking It*, Oren, UT: Empowering People Books, Tapes & Videos, 1990.

Losoncy, Lewis, *You Can Do It*, Englewood Cliffs, NJ: Prentice-Hall, Inc., 1980.

Main, Frank, *Perfect Parenting and Other Myths*, Minneapolis, MN: CompCare Publications, 1986.

Manaster, Guy J. and Corsini, Raymond, *Individual Psychology*, Itasca, IL: F.E. Peacock Publishers, Inc., 1982.

McKay, Gary D., and Dinkmeyer, Don, *How You Feel Is Up to You*, San Luis Obispo, CA: Impact Publishers, 1994.

Messer, Mitchell H., Coronado-Bogdaniak, M.D., and Dillon, Linda J., *Managing Anger*, Chicago, IL: C.O.R.E. Publishing, 1993.

Nelsen, Jane, *Positive Discipline*, New York: Ballantine Books, 1981, 1987, 1996.

Nelsen, Jane, *Understanding: Eliminating Stress and Finding Serenity in Life and Relationships*, Rocklin, CA: Prima Publishing, 1988, 1997.

Nelsen, Jane, Duffy, Roslyn, and Erwin, Cheryl, *Positive Discipline for Preschoolers*, Rocklin, CA: Prima Publishing, 1994.

Nelsen, Jane, Duffy, Roslyn, Escobar, Linda, Ortolano, Kate, and Owen-Sohocki, Debbie, *Positive Discipline: A Teacher's A-Z Guide*, Rocklin, CA: Prima Publishing, 1993.

Nelsen, Jane, Erwin, Cheryl, and Delzer, Carol, *Positive Discipline for Single Parents*, Rocklin, CA: Prima Publishing, 1993.

Nelsen, Jane, Intner, Riki, and Lott, Lynn, *Positive Discipline for Parenting in Recovery*, Rocklin CA: Prima Publishing, 1996.

Nelsen, Jane and Lott, Lynn, *Positive Discipline for Teenagers*, Rocklin, CA: Prima Publishing, 1994.

Nelsen, Jane, Lott, Lynn, and Glenn, H. Stephen, *Positive Discipline: A-Z*, Rocklin, CA: Prima Publishing, 1993.

Nelsen, Jane, Erwin, Cheryl, and Duffy, Roslyn, *Positive Discipline: The First Three Years*, Rocklin, CA: Prima Publishing, 1998.

Nelsen, Jane, Lott, Lynn, and Glenn, H. Stephen, *Positive Discipline in the Classroom*, Rocklin, CA: Prima Publishing 1997.

Pew, W.L., and Terner, J., *Courage to Be Imperfect*, New York: Hawthorn Books, 1978.

Platt, John and Owens, Dan, *Kids Study Groups, From Classroom Meetings to Peer Counseling*, Chicago, IL: Alfred Adler Institute of Chicago, 1981.

Platt, John, *Life in the Family Zoo*, Sacramento, CA, Dynamic Training 7 Seminars, Inc., 1989.

Popkin, Michael H., *Active Parenting Handbook*, Atlanta, GA: Active Parenting, Inc., 1983.

Schnebly, Lee, *Out of Apples*, Tucson, AZ: Manzanas Press, 1984.

Schnebly, Lee, *Do It Yourself Happiness*, Tucson, AZ: Manzanas Press, 1987.

Schnebly, Lee, *How to Be Your Own Counselor*, Tucson, AZ: Manzanas Press, 1987.

Stapleton, Jean and Bright, Richard, *Equal Marriage*, Nashville, TN: Abingdon, 1976.

Taylor, John F., *Helping Your Hyperactive Attention Deficit Child*, Rocklin, CA: Prima Publishing, 1990.

Taylor, John F., *Person to Person: Awareness Techniques for Counselors, Group Leaders and Parent Educators*, Saratoga, CA: R&E Publishers, 1984.

About the Authors

From left to right: Barbara Mendenhall, Riki Intner, Lynn Lott

Lynn Lott is a sought-after therapist, motivational speaker, frequent TV talk show guest, and prolific writer. She has written many books, five manuals for teachers and parent educators, and has contributed articles to numerous magazines, newspapers, and online publications.

Riki Intner is a marriage and family therapist in private practice and a trainer of parent educators. Riki serves on the board of the North American Society of Adlerian Psychology and is active in the Rotary. Riki is co-author of four self-help books, and her articles appear in various local publications. She has also contributed to several parenting manuals.

Barbara Mendenhall is a marriage, family, and child counselor in private practice and Executive Director of Family Education Centers in Sonoma County, California. She trains parents, teachers, and therapists on how to create encouraging environments at home and in the classroom. She has taught at Sonoma State University, the University of California San Diego, and the Santa Rosa Junior College. Barbara's articles on parenting and children appear regularly in local publications.

Index